Faith
in Conflict

CARLYLE MARNEY

FAITH in CONFLICT

NEW YORK • NASHVILLE • ABINGDON PRESS

FAITH IN CONFLICT

Copyright © MCMLVII by Abingdon Press

Library of Congress Catalog Card Number: 57-6119

SET UP, PRINTED, AND BOUND BY THE
PARTHENON PRESS, AT NASHVILLE,
TENNESSEE, UNITED STATES OF AMERICA

TO

VICTOR

who agreed with me in **nothing**
and was my friend in everything

"Oh, the contradictions, the contradictions!" Victor said to me that last day looking out over the canyon. "How could I become a believer after Lidice and London, Hamburg and Cologne, Nagasaki and Hiroshima?"

CONTENTS

After the storm we rested
in the winter sun at Bright Angel
and met *The Dragon;*
up by the monument, after several miles
in heavy snow (the tame deer?),
we saw *The Serpent;*
and next day before the log fire in the lounge,
snowbound from our dividing highways,
The Falcon and *The Vulture* came alive.
But our words were fragile symbols
and went away. Perhaps on paper
the encounter is more abiding.

FAITH and the DRAGON

On the porch at Bright Angel Lodge we rested in the winter sun after the ordeal of our drive through the hours of blizzard. The elements had howled and tugged at us across a hundred miles of high plateau, but now we were safe, quiet, warm in our blanketed lounge chairs. The high deck overlooked miles of drifted snow, white against the green of the timber, bounded by jagged lines from the distant peaks, and we dozed.

"It is almost like Switzerland," Ena said, and we talked. At peace, the war many days away, the odor of Victor's fine British tobacco rose like incense, and we talked.

How did it get so serious, so swiftly? And why have we kept up a conversation by letter these years? There really is such a difference between us. Of what could we really speak?

I remember we talked of the Dragon first. He was the monster who fed the flames of the war that kept so many so far from home. We talked of war, and tools for war, of matériel, and armaments, and that strange new power the British and the Americans hinted at. And then it became a more intimate encounter, and before we knew it, Scientism and Faith *were on opposite sides. But soon it was dinnertime, and with prime roast ribs before us, we forgot it—*

And yet, I cannot.

11

FAITH AND THE DRAGON

Science and reason have been made dragons
at which believing Don Quixotes
tilt with blunted lances.
There is no victory for me
in "believing the unbelievable."
Faith is victorious only
through the thrust of a personal encounter.

FOR EVEN AS A BOY you know of the conflict. In your jumbled-up version of things in general you know that across the mountain down at Dayton they are prosecuting a high-school teacher named Darwin or Darrow or something like that for teaching something about science, and it is all very, very bad. You try to read the *Knoxville Sentinel* by yourself, and you discover that the teacher is not Charles Darwin. It seems that Darwin is the lawyer, and this fellow Darrow wrote a book a man named Bryan doesn't like, or some such. But you hear your elders talk, and it comes straight at last: Charles Darwin isn't even at the trial, they tell you. He's

13

dead, already; and besides, the schoolteacher isn't Darrow; it's a boy named Scopes, but the big news is the lawyer fellow Darrow. You see his picture in the paper, and he looks a little like the John Barrymore you sneak off to watch on Saturday afternoons, but really he is more like the woodcut of the devil in a book called *Faust* you have thumbed through at the manse next door.

Yet in spite of your first impression that Darrow is the devil, everything is going to turn out all right for Jesus because a great white-maned knight named William Jennings Bryan is coming to the rescue of your home, your Bible, and the church where you go on Sundays.

But you keep trying to read the papers, and in your grand-dad's *Cincinnati Post* you discover that the white knight has been made to look foolish by Darwin-Darrow, the dragon. You decide for yourself that the knight is saying things he cannot prove, and because everybody you know is pulling for the white knight, you begin to feel sorry for the dragon.

Then, one day, the knight goes back to the lodge, eats his usual mammoth dinner, drinks a gallon of ice water, and dies right in the middle of his nap. You begin to suspect that he was not a knight at all, but was really more like the Don Quixote in your picture book who tilted at a dragon windmill he did not understand. You resolve to understand this dragon business, but it throws you for years into a crisis of confusion. And your dreams are filled with the scientific dragon Darrow and his conflict with your Don Quixotic faith.

Then, one day, in your own confusion on the edge of adulthood you come face to face with the mystery. Here your dragon science has no more an answer than your bumbling

14

faith has had, for you are standing on the lip of the ultimate mystery, the "impenetrable," Einstein called it. You approach the "human-boundary situation" where man reaches and knows his limit, and you cannot find any answer. Your science only halloos faintly as he goes in looking for a "what," but a budding and deeper faith begins to prompt you to look for a "who." Meantime there is

THE CRISIS OF CONFUSION

One net result of that six-hundred-year petty warfare between "men of science" and "men of religion"—currently and temporarily bereft of purpose by the shock of Nagasaki— is this crisis of confusion. Men of this generation cannot remember when Western civilization did not resemble an ant-hill into which enough hot water had been poured to stir things up generally. Men have always been seekers—looking for that city with foundations—how else any sort of civilization? But by and large, we are so much better at seeking than we are at finding that a kind of frantic confusion obscures for us that which we have been seeking. Some of us seek all our lives and never find.

It is pointless to try to indicate the scope of confusion's crisis. Everything is involved; all is affected. We spend our years caught in it, protesting it, able to describe and descry it, but not to evade it. For we have been taught by "functionalism" to find our place in the confusion and trust the "modern mind" to perform Messiah's service. But the "modern mind" cannot help us. Today's mind, omniverous, has, as someone says, mental indigestion and is laid up. Not with the gout of overindulged old age, but with the throbbing, pulsing ache of overdistended and greedy-eyed middle age. The modern mind cannot help, for the modern mind cannot digest that which fills it so full it cannot contract and expand.

It was good for the sash to be thrown up to let the musty medieval odors out so that the bracing winds of a stirring young spirit of freedom could sweep the corners. But the sash stuck! The bracing winds became a booming gale and along with musty dust blew out the draperies and the light, and without the light not even illusion is left, much less majestic faith. And the winds blew and the floods came and beat upon the house, and there came in the world-wide phenomenon of atheism.

Even the patron saint of Teutonic chauvinism, the Emperor Frederick II, caught the spirit of "research." He sealed an underling in a wine cask and waited for his spirit to depart by suffocation. No soul fragments appeared when the cask was broken, so the splendid conclusion of Frederick's logic was, "See, brethren, there is no soul!" [1] Such a spirit of pragmatic inquiry took off on wings of the morning and now across the centuries bears fruit in terms of *faith-proof atheists,* drowned like Barbarossa by the weight of their own armor in such little rivers. Psychiatric clinics are swelled to waiting-list proportions by emancipated women sent in part by Christian ministers who must know the lingo of neurosis, too. World-weary veterans of the educational factories and the wars sit in pastors' studies and do not know they are using Dostoevsky's words when they say, in effect, "Now, I am living out my life

[1] G. G. Coulton, *Medieval Panorama* (New York: The Macmillan Co., 1944), p. 447.

in my corner, taunting myself with the spiteful and useless consolation that an intelligent man cannot become any-thing . . . , and it is only the fool who becomes anything." [2] They pounce with pathetic sense of discovery on the words of Zarathustra, "Could it be possible! The old saint in the forest had not heard it?—that God is dead?" [3] They do not know that Nietzsche's God was like himself, made in Nietzsche's image, suffering and tortured. They look at you over their confessed sin waiting for this "reverend-prop-of-virtue" to begin breathing his "divine donkeyism."

Will Durant says that Australian aborigines swam under water and, breathing through reeds, pulled ducks beneath the surface by the legs and held them till their struggles ceased.[4] So this phenomenal enemy, atheism, child of misunderstood reason, does to ours and to us.

Nor has the crisis of confusion known any dissipation through the counterthrusting of the men of religion. The Paduanese theologian who dared not look through Galileo Galilei's telescope for fear that he might see what he could not believe has many compeers. Many "religious" claims have been utterly unjustifiable and have been as nonsensical as the ancient practice of sending a message to the dead by teaching the words to a slave just before his head was lopped off.[5]

---

[2] *Notes from Underground.* Reprinted from *The Short Novels of Dostoevsky* edited by Thomas Mann. Copyright 1945 by The Dial Press.

[3] Friedrich Nietzsche, *Thus Spake Zarathustra* in *The Philosophy of Nietzsche* (New York: The Modern Library, 1937), p. 27.

[4] *The Story of Civilization,* Vol. I, *Our Oriental Heritage* (New York: Simon & Schuster, Inc., 1935), p. 7.

[5] *Ibid.*

17

Nevertheless, man will not give up his search. Even in confusion he searches. And Dostoevsky's Father Zossima knew that for the humble Russian peasant it was the most important thing in the world to find something holy before which he could fall down and worship. The peasants knew, as all wish they might know, that "somewhere on earth there is someone, holy and exalted. He has the truth; . . . it will come one day to us, too, and rule over all the earth according to the promise." [6] In his confusion how wistfully man searches. Even among those who place credence no longer in any expression of the religion of their fathers, there is this wistfulness, this sense of something missing that should be eternally present. Yes, says Walter Marshall Horton, "this *is* an age of skepticism, cynicism and disillusionment; but it is also, and simultaneously, an age that is wistfully in quest of religious sustenance and religious certitude, and almost pathetically credulous when given half a chance." [7] Some writer, perhaps E. P. Dickie, has put it clearly when he says that in all of us there is a "real longing, however dim . . . . for the sound of a voice from above, some authentic Word of God." I saw it myself, dimly seen, in an epileptic friend of mine. How fully he tried to receive the preacher's word, but at home his God could speak to him only through an imitation turtle and a plastic moon.

But over all this personal confusion sits the Great Dragon to little faith, Doubt, made by misunderstood science and displaced reason, scientism.

---

[6] *The Brothers Karamazov*, tr. Constance Garnett (New York: Random House), p. 27.

[7] *Theism and the Modern Mood* (New York: Harper & Bros., 1930), p. 10.

THE FIELD OF SCIENCE—ITS THRUST

Whatever else the general field of science is, it is *convincing*. I have not heard any so-called *religieux* denying atomic theories, have you? Nagasaki and Hiroshima, whatever they were morally, were intellectually convincing. Within this eternally exploding universe the toolmaker, though made Lilliputian by his own discoveries and tools, by some subterranean urge at last threatens to become his own superman. It is not strange to Bertrand Russell that "every man would like to be God if it were possible." [8] And it is precisely in the field of scientific inquiry that man has found it most difficult to admit the impossibility. For man, the biped who stands up straight, the toolmaker, is also always and incurably the questioner, the searcher, the critic. Once he inquires, no longer can he be mere spectator. He becomes participant in the search—a scientist. It is out of the eternal *how* and *why,* out of the restless search, out of the brooding "I will, I will, I will ascend," out of the impelling urge "to know," that science is born.

Birth is all that is necessary for an Amazon. The degree of growth is hardly a problem. Caesonia was born big and had her court from the beginning [9]—so science. As has ever been true with courts and royalty, claims were made in the name of the royal one that royalty would never have made, so with this royal tool—science. She would never claim the exclusive right of domain some of her hangers-on have claimed for her. When science speaks for herself, she speaks

[8] *Power, a New Social Analysis* (New York: W. W. Norton & Co., 1938), p. 11

[9] Made empress by Caligula because of her tremendous size, A.D. 40.

out of her true nature recognizing her limitations as does any royal lady. Those who fear her and those who fawn upon her have created the dragon she never meant to be.

Everything belongs to science! [10] But art and religion are joint proprietors. There is no fact of experience which the scientist will not claim as part of his data, but so does art, and so does religion. The difference is a thing of attitude. To this common field of fact the man of science comes to observe and measure, the man of art to admire and reproduce or express, the man of religion to have communion and worship.

The scientific attitude is a value judgment based on a realistic metaphysic. The most worthy facts to science are those most clearly and accurately observable, measurable, countable. The most real is the most measurable. Science has no choice with respect to materialism; its matter *is* matter. By the same token the scientific method and certainty are a material method and a material certainty. The tools of the scientific method are mathematical equations, logical rules, calculation, observation, analysis, reasoning, testing by induction, and demonstration. While a junior physicist at Oak Ridge, my young brother was set to plotting a curve on the radioactivity of certain materials according to exposure time. When he returned the problem to his director, he was asked how many points he had used to determine the graph of the curve. He replied in terms of hundreds but was told to

[10] In this discussion I have drawn heavily on a splendid short book by John MacMurray, *The Structure of Religious Experience* (New Haven, Conn.; Yale University Press, 1936).

report when his observations determining the curve numbered in thousands! For the scientific attitude is based on what Leibniz termed *vérités du fait*. Fact is the thing! Matters of will and personality and what Frederick baron Corvo calls the "personal equation" [11] are ever excluded. One must "sit down before fact as a little child." [12] One must follow meekly to whatever conclusion observable fact leads; the desire of the heart and the will of the creature have no standing; facts are guiding stars.[13] Following hard on *vérités du fait* are *vérités de raison,* but by these rational guides the observer must always be logico-mathematical. He must trust nothing that defies touch, measurement, or proof. In Goethe's *Faust,* Mephistopheles describes this rational certainty:

> Herein your learned men I recognize?
> What you touch not, miles distant from you lies;
> What you grasp not, is naught in sooth to you;
> What you count not, cannot you deem be true;
> What you weigh not, that hath for you no weight;
> What you coin not, you're sure is counterfeit.

The influences of science and reason, strangely enough, occur to our minds in terms of living personality, the one entity defying scientific analysis. Some great personalities form foci around which revolve the mass of claims and discoveries and theories that form the scientific influence. From

---

[11] *A History of the Borgias* (New York: The Modern Library, 1931), Preface, p. xvi.

[12] Huxley to Charles Kingley.

[13] See E. P. Dickie, *Revelation and Response* (New York: Chas. Scribner's Sons, 1938), pp. 71 ff.

21

this vantage point those minds are these: [14] Charles Darwin, Albert Einstein; Friedrich Nietzsche, Sigmund Freud; Karl Marx, John Dewey. The influence of each is best expressed in terms of the inroads made by the ideas, theories, and discoveries of each upon some previously established basic concept. The influence of each is most clearly seen in terms of the breakdown, the overthrow, or the partial deterioration of some comparatively unchallenged frame of thought:

Charles Darwin: The breakdown of the concept of man as the biological aristocrat. Man is made of the same stuff as all else *organic.*

Albert Einstein: The breakdown of the organic-inorganic concept of life matter. Stuff is stuff, same stuff, and matter is energy.

Friedrich Nietzsche: The breakdown of the governance of mind and spirit. Life is the thing! Life force is what matters, and the great Man is the plaything of *impulse and instinct.*

Sigmund Freud: The breakdown of the rule of the conscious. Rule is *in the hands of the unconscious.*

Karl Marx: The breakdown of the conceptual worth of the individual. *Society matters alone.*

John Dewey: The breakdown of personality as the prime factor in civilizing mankind. *The function is the object,* not the functioner.

[14] But see Chapter III for a wider listing that includes the sources from which these came.

Science, "superfluous luxury," [15] "impatient daughter, who claims her heritage while her mother still lives," [16] is always *tool* and never craftsman; always *method,* never master. Where science speaks of herself, she admits this and glories in it. Unkind friends, blundering disciples, joyfully forsaking the one-time queen Theology, crowned her divine, to her discomfiture, for science knew she was handmaid. Science knows, has always known, that without craftsman there is no need for tool, that without the physicist there is no physics. Personality is paramount. Without it the laws of mathematics remain, but who would need them? This is the justification for the claim that the field of religion (personal relations) encloses and limits the field of science. Certain thinkers have followed only the banners of science, unaware that no tool can save the world, since tools must serve—not command.

Science—like everything else—is subject to the laws of development. A watchword for her banners now is "exactness." Follow wherever observable truth leads. Hear and obey this maxim: "If you miss the first button hole, you will not succeed in buttoning up your coat!" Be sane! Follow what you see! And on the whole, science is sane. But it was not always so! For science arises in the pattern, in response to the same urges, and in dread of the same mysteries as does her "mother"—religion. She is, on the whole, subject to the same basic explanation in terms of her ancestral beginnings, and in her childhood there are traces of identical fantasies. John

[15] Dostoevsky, *Notes from Underground,* p. 144.
[16] Salomon Reinach, *Orpheus, a History of Religions* (New York: Liveright Publishing Corp., 1929), p. 33.

MacMurray has pointed out that only a moment ago in humanity's chronology science was bending all her efforts to find the elixir of life, and the consuming quest of the best was for the philosopher's stone to transmute base metals to gold. Even Sir Isaac Newton cherished this desire—and realized it centuries before the atomic explorers transmuted their heavy atoms to government gold. For Sir Isaac the method was much simpler, however. He merely transferred from the laboratory to an office—that of head of his Majesty's mint!

The curse of having to wait for development limits even Amazon! How irksome to human nature to have to grow before looking over the garden walls on tiptoe. But here, even science must submit to the limitations of stature and wait for growth to bring height and depth.

Science—halted by dependence on progress—is limited in her scope. By her very nature she must measure tangibles. She recognizes no other dispensation. But unhappily for her disciples, almost all that really matters to human personality is *intangible*. All tangibles perish. Nothing visible remains. The grinding wheels of the inexorable are set to crush all that can collapse. *Only the perishable is measurable! Only the malleable is provable!* There is almost nothing of enduring value in human life that science can prove; Happiness, freedom, equality, freedom of the will, world co-operation: these eternals are demonstrable only in terms of faith and human action.[17] Every important thing in human life lies somewhere outside the sphere of the mathematically calculable: the soul,

[17] Lin Yutang, *Between Tears and Laughter* (New York: John Day Co., Inc., 1943), pp. 74-77.

God, decency, self-respect, honesty, pride, hatred, fear, revenge, sadism, personal ambition, love, loyalty, devotion, forgiveness, confidence, trust, self-sacrifice. The formula and the test tube, the equation and the slide rule, are cold. The crucible is heated, but artificially. Life is, of itself, warm. Analyzing the component parts into slivers of wood, varnish, ivory, catgut, and glue can never explain the vibrancy of viola—nor, as Lin Yutang says, can reducing high c to a certain number of vibrations ever explain Lily Pons.

Science—even in her own bailiwick—is limited. Gifted at saying "how," she seldom can say "why" or "wherefore." Lin Yutang with characteristic and charming Oriental candor lists something of her weakness here: Science explains how the atoms behave—but not why they so behave. It describes how two molecules of sodium and carbon come together—but does not explain why they must. Science describes acids and alkalis—but cannot say anything about the ultimate acidity of acids. It proves that quinine kills malaria germs—but does not know why. Before the ultimate door of Mystery science must stop. It observes and proves the survival of the fittest— but cannot account for the arrival of the fittest. It explains the survival value of the giraffe's long neck—but cannot explain the first long neck, or the leopard's spots, or the flower's fragrance. Ultimately, it seems, bees just produce honey, and cows just make milk, and lilacs just create out of the common sod that unmistakable, incomparable perfume—and they all do it simply, finally, and inevitably! [18]

"If there were nothing in man but what the chemist and

---

[18] *Ibid.,* p. 76 rearranged, slightly condensed.

the biologist can discover, there would be no chemistry and no biology." [19] Obviously, there is little point in being a materialist if no one knows what matter is. Kant said materialism shatters on the humblest earthworm.

THE FIELD OF RELIGION—ITS THRUST

The field of fact is the same for science and religion,[20] but the centers of interest are different. The concern of science is *utilitarian;* that of religion is *personal.* The field of religion is the whole field of common experience organized in relation to the primary fact of persons in relationship. In all the rubbings together of personality man is in the religious arena. There is no relationship outside it, for that is what religion is all about—communion, contact between persons, fellowship. The stuff of science is matter—hence science is material. The stuff of religion is communion—hence religion is spiritual.

No two people can live together in any human relationship outside the realm of religion. Husband and wife, parent and child, comrades-in-arms, employer and workman, teacher and learner, seller and buyer, judge and defendant, all are living in religion's field. Even the vocabulary those relationships force on mankind is the vocabulary of religion, and the relationship involved can continue only by the constant use of such religious words as confession, repentance, forgiveness, reconciliation, and atonement. Nor can any human relation-

[19] Dickie, *op. cit.,* p. 27. Used by permission of Charles Scribner's Sons and T. & T. Clark.
[20] Attention is again called to MacMurray's brilliant analysis *The Structure of Religious Experience.*

ship be broken except by the use of religious terms: trespass, infidelity, wrath and pride, usury and lust. And even when death causes severance, the terms then used are purely religious, indeed; there is no other field within which we can express ourselves, for even doubt, atheism, and nihilism are religious terms.

The task of religion is the realization of fellowship between persons on the highest possible level. The religious intention includes the scientific and the artistic, for fellowship on the highest possible level cannot ignore the utilitarian and the aesthetic. The great goal of religion is the entry into perfect communion with the Great Other. As its corollary appears always the task of the maintenance of human community. And religion is the only means, for it only deals exclusively in terms of the personal. As the religious intention unfolds, it is seen to be the achieving of a universal reconciliation between persons: between I and Thou, between all I's and all others called thou; between I, my self—and the One felt to be Other—between all I's and all others called thou—and *The Great Thou*. This is the redemption of the world.

If a man wishes (as many do) to escape the thought and claims of religion, he can do it. But in order to do it, he must reject completely the consciousness that he belongs to any community of persons. He must seek a hermithood without *any* earthly communication with persons, must become Automaton, *sans* love, for who would be lover? *sans* pride, for to whom could he boast? *sans* warmth, for there is no friend; *sans* laughter, for nonsense comes from communion, too; and *sans* tears, for only persons are tragic—and funny—and *sans*

27

joy, for there would be no children. The only way to reject
religion is to deny or forget our relationship to any other.

A high-sounding claim comes down ex cathedra through
certain self-styled intimates of the high priests of the cult of
misunderstood reason: "Religion," it says here, "belongs to
mankind's earlier stages and will be superseded as human
development goes on." Stuff and nonsense! Granted gladly
that it is to be hoped, fervently, that many forms and expressions of religion will be left along the road (for the
friends of religion do her more harm than any enemy), to
say we will leave the whole vehicle behind is to talk foolish-
ness. That could be true only if we were all hatched by
incubation and lived on the underside of rocks, existing—
dying—without ever the consciousness of any other. But this
world is a world of *persons,* and the "same leaky bottom in
these wild waters bears us all." And that is religion's business.

The world of fact for reason and science is the world of
fact for religion. It is a real world—in which, amidst our
knowing and doubting, sharing and keeping, loving and
hating, achieving and denying, releasing and frustrating, religion is firmly rooted in our race-wide common experience.
Because faith and reason have been made to seek each the
other's birthright, it is now and has been a truism that for a
thinking man *religion adds more burdens than it removes.*
That is to say, religion, as commonly understood, imposes
such a burden of "believing the unbelievable" that many an
"average" intelligence has found the freedom from believing
"unbelievables" as afforded by skepticism and doubt to be

vastly more attractive than the freedom from anxiety promised by religion, as commonly understood.

Nor is this to insinuate for a moment that no "unbelievables" are to be found in the arena of science and reason. G. B. Shaw is, as usual, quite lucid on this point:

> Science is [not] free from legends, witchcraft, miracles, biographic boostings of quacks as heroes and saints, and of barren scoundrels as explorers and discoverers. On the contrary, the iconography and hagiology of Scientism are as copious as they are mostly squalid.[21]

Yet to say that much religious matter adds more burden than its acceptance would remove is to admit that a great many religious leaders have made a claim science would never have made: *That the truth of a principle or idea depends upon the acceptance* in toto *of the literary framework in which it is preserved.*

As Shaw again puts it, and to make the same point,

> No student of science has yet been taught that specific gravity consists in the belief that Archimedes jumped out of his bath and ran naked through the streets of Syracuse shouting Eureka, Eureka, or that the law of inverse squares must be discarded if anyone can prove that Newton was never in an orchard in his life.[22]

But from this point of view it seems quite plain that both the "form critics" of the last century and their opponents have focused such emphatic concern on the literary frame-

[21] *Back to Methuselah*, "A Lesson from Science to the Churches," Preface. Used by permission of The Public Trustee and The Society of Authors.
[22] *Ibid.*

29

work of revealed truth that religion, forgetting the God-made task of reason, has been forced into the position by her friends of claiming to stand upon interpretations she never held and monstrosities she never sponsored. For without the inexorable pressure and scrutinizing light of reason, religion descends to the level of the unbelievable gullibly received, the opiate of waking minds, the panacea of the unthinking— and faith? She becomes either a dodo bird or an ostrich.

When faith is either—dodo or ostrich—then the church teaches what Shaw says some do: *that* the world was made in 4004 B.C.; *that* damnation means an eternity of blazing brimstone; *that* the Immaculate Conception means that sex is sinful and that Christ was parthenogenetically brought forth by a virgin descended in like manner from a line of virgins right back to Eve; *that* the Trinity is an anthropomorphic monster with three heads which are yet only one head; *that* in Rome the bread and wine on the altar become flesh and blood, and in England in a still more mystical manner they do and they do not; *that* the Bible is an infallible scientific manual; *that* we may lie and cheat and murder and then wash ourselves innocent in the blood of the lamb on Sunday at the cost of a credo and a penny in the plate, and so on.[23] There is no salvation, not even civilization, in a reasonless religion crude enough to expect belief of such things or, as the same writer puts it, "irreligious enough to believe that such belief constitutes a religion."

Religion cannot appeal to imagination, heart, and spirit while leaving mind behind—not and be whole! By the same

[23] *Ibid.*, "The Danger of Reaction," Preface.

30

token the content of religious belief will not be contained by reason—not and be religion! But religion must tax thought if it would develop mind;

it is the problems which most imperiously appeal to the reason for solution which open those glimpses into the secret of the universe that most fascinate the heart and awe the imagination. . . . Unless religion be an external challenge to the reason it can have no voice for the imagination, and no value for the heart.[24]

On the other hand, no one has put it more succinctly than Dickie when he says, "The task of reason is to make impossible all religions save the best." [25]

And the gadfly has been at work! Not, principally, as *Formgeschichte* on the literary vehicle of revelation, but without doubt, the Bible and its place have been quite radically affected by the stingings of reason. The result is to give to seeking mankind an infinitely more real, a positively more valuable, and an intrinsically more precious record of man's search and God's gracious dealings in his revelatory encounters. Relieved of the encrusting claims plastered to its thrilling pages by the tendency of believing man to create his own receptacle for holding the external proof of his belief, freed from its aloof altar where, worshiped as *das Werden-in-sich*, it was, for many, more magic and superstition than record of a living way, it (the Bible) can now take its place at the living crossroads, record of a lived way, with answers that did work, do work, and will work for seeking man. Free,

[24] Andrew M. Fairbairn, *The Philosophy of the Christian Religion* (New York: The Macmillan Co., 1949), p. 5.
[25] *Op. cit.*, p. 112.

now, since reason has been at work, to become *das Wort Gottes* for my seeking heart.

It no longer has to stop hemorrhages of the nose! Though, like a Kentucky friend of mine, some may still turn in such moments of crisis to Ezekiel and proclaim earnestly, "Smite with thine hand, and stamp with thy foot, and say, Alas . . . !" blaming the failure to stop spouting blood on little faith rather than on the inefficacy of the Scripture as a nosebleed stopper. But the Book does not keep its place by such bygone efficacies. Nor does the Bible now have to stop spent bullets from striking soldiers' hearts. Many a soldier learned that belt buckles and decks of cards would also deflect spent slugs. And, surely, not even the manufacturers of the little metal-backed New Testaments for use in soldiers' breast pockets in time of war believed that such thin armor would turn an 180 grain slug with a muzzle velocity of 2,710 feet per second and 2,940 pounds of knock-down power, not at anything like killing range! Now, reason has said: The Bible no longer must stop bleeding noses or spent slugs. It does not have to speak about the N.R.A. blue eagle, or low-pressure tires, or tank warfare, or Hitler's mystic number, or the size of Satan's pants. It is now free, and largely by the thrustings of reason, to do what God gave it to do:

1. *To teach searching man that he is competent and terribly responsible for his own dealings with God without whom he is lost in his own infinity of lostness, the Self; and*

2. *To show how and where and in whom this competent, responsible man may find that Other whom having not seen he knows to be awfully and eternally there.*

32

Let me put it more bluntly—as Emil Brunner says it: The Bible reveals *Gott-zum-Menschen-hin* (God who approaches man) and *Menschen-von-Gott-her* (man who comes from God).[26] That is the mission, and reason has helped us get it back.

Nor is the task of reason that of mere critic. When reason has dealt with the literary framework of religion, reducing all that can be reduced, the emergent remnant, the primal deposit, the elemental part (reduced to form and made evident by the action of reason, the catalyst) still needs the prodding presence of reason, the gadfly.

Given: God. Given: Man. The problem: communion—and how to bring it about. Here reason speaks to help revelation. Who is God?—and lo! a theology appears. What is man? The answer is an anthropology. How can he be what he is not? This demands a soteriology. And reason helps! But she can neither confine nor contain. Too much is asked of her. She cannot demonstrate that which she cannot comprehend. Often, like the Copernican monk, she cannot admit that which she will not see. She cannot allow what she cannot assimilate, and from her high perch often croaks "untrue" about that which is nevertheless happening out of her sight in the next room. Reason can strip, deny, taunt, deride, test, disprove, provoke, stimulate, and limit—but she cannot destroy! Always, and sometimes so hauntingly, "it" is there. "It"? The possibility, the probability, nay, even the actuality, of relationship between the *I* and the *Other*.

[26] *The Divine-Human Encounter* (Philadelphia: The Westminster Press, 1943), p. 47.

33

"Since I have become a Christian, there are moments when I am tormented by doubt that all of it is so. When I was an unbeliever, I was tormented always by fear that some of it was so!"

Meanwhile, the great dragon, Doubt, between forays sits and wipes his snout. In his great paunch, still undigested, the edible fragments of his latest spoilage lie fermenting, until the gas that burns from dragon nostrils rises to send this fire breather after other little Don Quixotes. His name is Doubt; his function—to destroy; his joy—to maim; his enemy—Faith; his pedigree: *Doubt,* out of the filly *Science,* who never ran her own race (by the sire *Lucifer,* who only wanted to run but being a dragon had to fly) and whose grandam is *Reason,* who also ran but never finished. It is late in our day—nearly A.D. 2000—and the great dragon, Doubt—sits—and watches—

God is given! And the dragon spits! Prove him! Prove him? Weigh him, test him, analyze him, delineate him! Do it, if you can, teleologically, ontologically, cosmologically, anthropologically, and still you cannot see him, nor can I. But faith keeps shouting that he is *there* waiting for the encounter he has always willed should come.

THE THRUST OF A PERSONAL ENCOUNTER

Encounter is always drama—often tragedy, more often comedy, but always drama. Any encounter is drama—for drama implies action, doing! It is only in the realm of drama —of doing—that religion and thought can evade for a time metaphysic. It is just here that religious experience can demonstrate its validity. It lies in the validity of the drama—the act—

34

the event—something that has happened. The event, the drama, the act, like everything dramatic (as opposed to metaphysic) has definite denouement. It begins; it has characters who either are controlling the action (caravan) or are caught in the action (carrousel); it rises to the high point of encounter, then subsides to its tragic, comic, tragico-comical, or romantico-heroic conclusion. Encounter involves, as drama, two factors—*characters* and connecting *action*. Otherwise there is no encounter, but a juxtaposition of blind forces, personless and valueless, in contra-operation.

The gospel claim is that something has happened! It tells of an encounter—*the* encounter. To use Brunner's clear phrases, "God-who-approaches-man" has encountered "man-who-comes-from-God." This makes Christianity happen. It is deed, act, word, drama, *encounter*.[27] Its reproduction is the only vital religious experience, and this event is man's only hope. Man, the one who comes from God, can and does meet the God who is anxious to be known. Man, the finite, can encounter the infinite. Man, the limited, can enter relationship with the illimitable. I can know Other!

The claim is breathtaking in its very audacity. Metaphysic cannot explain it, reason cannot accept it, science cannot comprehend it, and most of the time religion herself does not know how to convey it. Experience only can validate it and having validated can scarcely find words to portray it. Only in drama can it be expressed. The Encounter happens! *Man* comes to terms with *Ultimatus*. *I* meets *Thou*. And who is

---

[27] *Ibid.,* chs. ii, iii.

this "being" [28] who comes to such an encounter? He is, first of all,

Man, zoon,

the mammal, a warm-blooded creature who comes from one egg, a creature of biology, heredity, and eugenics. He is the result of the physical union of cells and the laws of cell-divisive growth while nurtured with genes and hormones in the warm wet womb of the mothering organism—herself zoon. Man is the living one who lives unseeing, untasting, unknowing, in the dark, until he becomes

homo-anthropos.

Then he is the man who stands up straight, the only one who stands up straight, until in middle age he begins to need various and sundry braces and girdles to hold him together at the seams. He is the man who sees and feels and has dominion, the creature who knows and responds to climate and hunger, earth and water and fire and food and clothing. Man, the geographer, is also *homo-amplius,* man the grand, grandest of zoon, the dominator, who is

homo-faber.

Man is the maker, the craftsman, the master of environment, the engineer. What marvelous and monstrous engines he has engineered from that first stick he still holds in his hand! Man, the toolmaker, the master-mechanic, the research physicist, the bio-organico-in-

[28] See Emil Brunner, *Man in Revolt* (Philadelphia: The Westminster Press, 1947), Intro., chs. i, ii, iii.

organico-chemist, the astronomer-mathematician, the navigator, the carpenter who digs even his grave holes with mathematical precision, is always and everywhere *homo-creator.*

Man is the creator whose will to be what he is not drives him to fashion what he has dreamed. For man, *homo-desidero,* the desirer, the one who longs, longs until he makes—as maker, as creator out of nothing but idea, produces the realization of idea. He makes his own tools, a red to match the sun at eve, a piece of wood to sing like a bird, a bigger piece of wood to sound like rapids in a stream, and a piece of brass to sound like dawn coming up late or the cry of an evening. Out of it all comes his music, his pictures, his buildings, his ornaments, his language, his sculpture; for man the artisan is also man *the artist,* and well that he is, for it makes possible and better his lot as

homo-politicus—

homo-historicus. Man the social being is man who belongs to history and not only makes it but remembers it. Man is always and invariably social. Always *homo-sui-juris,* indeed, he is also and always *homo alieni juris.* Master of himself, he is always subject to some other—society. He is the creature of history and civics, literature and annals, government and institutions and schools. Everywhere he is the social one—the creature of sex, marriage, homes, law, business, power, war, legislative groups and, even among the ancients, labor unions and

37

fraternities, and secret orders, and burial associations. And there is more! Man could be these only by virtue of his being more. No one knows how long he has been

homo-sapiens—

homo-erector. Man is the wise one—man-with-his-mind-on-the-stretch — man-who-stands-up-straight-with-his-mind-on-tiptoe . . . *homo-interrogatus*—The questioner, the critic, until in advanced wisdom he becomes man the cynic! He is the one who asks and is crucified by his asking, the one who will not let sleeping dogs lie . . . who puts lights on the end of a stick so that he can see inside another's private stomach, who puts ears on a wire and listens to another's heart murmur. He is the one who sees a star and asks how big and how far. He is the one whose mind measures what mind cannot grasp—infinite horizon. He is the one who can—who must—deny, doubt, or believe. He is the creature of philosophy, theology, science, ethics, morals, law.

But there is more—much more! If there were no more, there would long ago have ceased to be community. *Homo-politicus-sapiens* cannot hold himself together in any enduring communion. There must be more, and there is. For man, everywhere you find him, is

homo-religiosus.

Always there is that real longing, however dimmed or embryonic, for the trumpet voice from outside, for that sound of a Word from the God. Even in his denials man is religious. He cannot evade his need or forget it. He has always some God or an idol,[29] even himself.

As *homo-religiosus* he may in moments of uplift be *homo-donum,* the giver, or *honoratus,* the honorable, or *fanaticus,* the mad. But he is the religious one, the only religious one always and inevitably; and even his madness is frequently a religious madness.

The crown, the dominator, the user and maker, the thinker, planner, builder, ruler, is also *the worshiper,* though often he worships a devil. He is *the seeker,* the one who desires communion. Is this all? It is enough! Enough to say that in this man there are all the qualities of Ultimatus to some degree. Who knows what man can become?

This is what I mean when I sum up all these embryonic ultimati to say that man is

homo-imago-dei—

man in the image of the Ultimate. He is the created one who creates, the built one who builds, the planned one who plans, the ruled one who rules, the thought one who thinks, the dominated one who dominates, the told one who tells, and the asked one who asks. He is man, the competent, responsible one, who must deal with Ultimatus for himself; he is man who is able, made for communion, able to commune, responsible for communion, the one who encounters God, Prot-arche, Primus Causus, Ultimatus, Pater, Saviour, Redentor, Alpha-Omega.

[29] Martin Luther.

"Fantastic!" cries Metaphysic. "Naïve!" smirks Intelligence. "Absurd mummery!" sniff Logic and Reason. "Salvation is incredible and irrelevant!" "Redemption is unnecessary and unthinkable!" But two things man cannot deny: communion and encounter; they are obverse sides of the same thing— *religion.*

There is no salvation for me in "believing the unbelievable." Neither dogma nor metaphysic offers any redemption for this race. Religion is a matter for persons, in persons, between persons. I am man-who-comes-from-God, and I find no peace until I meet him—until the *encounter happens.* Does it come by believing the unbelievable? Not a word of it! I do not lay my mind down to become a Christian. Ultimatus gave it to his image—me! But in that vast realm open to me, beyond epistemology, beyond semantics, beyond metaphysics, beyond logic and reason, beyond *l'horizon du rationale,* I encounter him in *faith.*

Faith? Now faith is the naïve acceptance of patterns unthinkable, the grotesque submission to unexamined concepts, the blind and undiscriminating reliance on dogmatic misconceptions. Never. That is, it never was, it never is, it never will be!

Let Brunner sum up encounter's thrust: When God meets man, Christian truth is born. This God who has chosen to deal with man does so by a deed, an act, encounter. God has done it! And he has never dealt with man except as encounter between concerned persons. In the Christ there is to be found both! God who approaches man, man who comes from God. Faith is man's responsible act in response to the Word. Obedience-in-trust is that total self-giving, that complete renunciation of one's own security, that utter dependence, that face to face relation possible only when one is face to face with one to whom one can afford to renounce himself. I become the possessed, the disposable, and stammeringly say—"My Lord!" I am affected, changed, no longer solitary, I have a Master, a Thou! [30]

In the thrust of my personal encounter the dragon does not go away—he is always there . . . but now he is a one-eyed owl —*I have a Thou!*

God, who desires to be Thou to the whole human race, wills to meet man.

How encounter? Will you hear a parable? Do you remember Cosette in *Les Misérables?* Alone in the dark she so dreaded, straining at the bucket of water she was forced to carry, unaware of the possibility of encounter, the redemption Valjean would bring—where better than here can we understand ourselves on the edge of our impenetrable mystery and the encounter that can come in the agony?

She had only one thought, to fly; to fly with all her might, across woods, across fields, to houses, to windows, to lighted candles. Her eyes fell upon the bucket. . . . She grasped the handle with both hands. She could hardly lift the bucket.

She went a dozen steps in this manner, but the bucket was full, it was heavy, she was compelled to rest it on the ground. . . . She walked bending forward, her head down, like an old woman: the weight of the bucket strained and stiffened her thin arms.

[30] See Brunner, *The Divine-Human Encounter,* ch. ii.

. . . .

Arriving near an old chestnut tree which she knew, . . . the poor little despairing thing could not help crying: "Oh! my God! my God!"

At that moment she felt all at once that the weight of the bucket was gone. A hand, which seemed enormous to her, had just caught the handle, and was carrying it easily. She raised her head. A large dark form, straight and erect, was walking beside her in the gloom. It was a man who had come up behind her, and whom she had not heard. This man, without saying a word, had grasped the handle of the bucket she was carrying.

. . . .

There are instincts for all the crises of life.
The child was not afraid.

Later, Victor Hugo says, the child learned to call him father and knew him by no other name.

The One who died, crossed, a companion to thieves, will not protest that in Jean Valjean I have found a parable of my encounter with him.

CHAPTER TWO

FAITH and the SERPENT

Victor, do you remember the monument to somebody or other on the lip of Grand Canyon where we stopped that second day? I don't know how many miles we had walked in the heavy snow, but even the fatigue was glorious. As we stopped in the little pocket where only winter sun could reach us, and looked at the unearthly mystery, white clad, down to the tropic belt below us in the canyon, who first mentioned the Serpent? What business had Evil to come there? Why did our talks always come so swiftly to ultimate questions?

"How can you speak so blithely of simple belief when we live in a world like this?" you thrust at me. Then, as if to yourself, added: "I have been to Lidice and Krakow. I had dear friends in both Coventry and Hamburg." And even there in the open, as in another upper room long ago, the chill wind from the presence of Evil crept in around us. But we went back to lunch and forgot it.

FAITH AND THE SERPENT

Whoever said that human nature has changed?
There is a world full of evil,
and I am involved.
Faith cannot answer evil
by watering down the fires of human nature.
But the personal encounter of faith
releases a transforming power.

YOU FIRST SAW THE SYMBOL of the serpent crudely chalked on the dark, dank wall of that underground room at first-grade school, and you knew of the presence of evil. For the serpent was associated with the ugly words that were more than "fools' names in public places" scrawled there for the whole world to read. Already you had behind you your first brush with corporate evil at the hands of wild little-boy gangs that were "after" you, had heard the curses and felt the shuddering blows that gaunt madman gave his team of great mules in the alley, had seen a high-school teacher carried out with a bloody head from a hammer thrown by a toughie. But you thought that this evil and this serpent were local characters; you did not know then that evil is everywhere.

You did not know then that the little blind boy who cried when the neighborhood cop brought him a red wagon had been blinded by somebody's syphilis. You had not yet tried to play pretend games with a long ward of little fellows burned and tortured by sins not their own, nor had you yet walked between long cot rows in that Asiatic orphanage while Father Chichetti tried to smile with you at the hoarded worthless objects treasured at each pillow by little derelicts who had nothing else to treasure. Nor had you then stood in a jeep to watch rice and cabbage measured out to swarms of ulcerated children outside that old prisoner camp near Tsuiki. You did not know, back there, that evil is everywhere, that the serpent is scrawled on all kinds of walls, even your own.

A while ago in Louisville a speaker was quoted as saying, "War, hate, and discord are fables; illness and pain are fables; health and ease are the facts!" Tell it to the Marines! Tell Bob Talley that it is a fairy tale that he left two good legs in Germany. Tell Euclid Johnson that evil is fable; he left half his eyes, most of his stomach, and sixty pounds of flesh in a prison camp on Bataan. Tell Bud Hauge it is a dream that the Chinese swarmed across the Yalu and left him lying on a tank tread dead from his armpits down. Tell the rent corpse of my boyhood friend that evil is a fable; his name is John, he was a colonel of paratroopers, they machine-gunned him in his chute straps in Belgium. Tell any prostitute that there is no discord. Shout down the sunken corridors of one of Poland's mass graves that there is

no real hate; tell any of the ghosts of the ten million starve-
lings that; or for that matter, tell any of these eighteen
thousand university students that, but don't try to take up
a collection! They know that pain and evil are not fables.
How on earth does such a plaintive, misanthrope child of
misread Neoplatonism survive to repeat itself in the hearts of
neurotic men and women? Let us be bold about it! Evil is
real, and faith must meet the serpent, must face the awful
fact of evil and the possibility of salvation from evil. Is the
tension between them the mainspring of the moral universe?
Is this tension a phase of a greater tension that holds the
whole of the cosmos in its place? Meanwhile, the man is torn
between his possibilities. Is this the meaning of Cross—
that something infinite is being pulled apart?

THE MIGHTY CONTRADICTION

Whatever the meaning of the tension it finds expression
not only in the whole of all societies but in the single man
in each society as well. In every man faith finds at the same
moment almost unlimited possibility for evil and for salvation. Drunken Fyodor Pavlovitch, delirious with joy over
his wife's death, shouted in the street, *"Lord, now lettest
Thou Thy servant depart in peace."* [1] Sir John Hawkins kid-
napped Negroes for the slave trade in his ship the "Jesus." [2]
The bereft Anne spits upon evil, crippled Richard, and he answers, "Never came *poison* from so *sweet* a place." [3] The

[1] Dostoevsky, *The Brothers Karamazov*, p. 6.
[2] W. Macneile Dixon, *The Human Situation* (New York: Longmans,
Green & Co., 1937), p. 99.
[3] *The Tragedy of King Richard the Third*, Act I, scene 2.

47

possibility for both poison and sweetness is in each of us; in each the possibility of either and both is well-nigh infinite. Dickie says it succinctly: "A correct estimate of man sees in him an extraordinary dignity conjoined with an extraordinary distress. He can rise to such heights as to justify our belief that he is made in the image of God; and he can descend far lower than the brute creation. The angel has him by the hand and the serpent by the heart."[4]

How is it that we are so made, as Sir John Hutton said it, "that when true religion goes out the window something else comes up from the drains?" How is it that in our hearts and in our Anglo-Saxon tongue "hallowed be thy name" and "heil der Fuehrer" have the same root? Dostoevsky points to the fact beyond dispute that "man likes to make roads and to create," "but why," he asks, "has he such a passionate love for destruction and chaos also?"[5] Is he instinctively afraid of completing his edifice, attaining his object? Why does he "grasp things worthless and leave what is precious behind him?"[6]

When faith lives with men, she becomes aware of the mighty contradiction that splits man down the middle, and then faith must learn a thing or two. Man the full, grand one is also and simultaneously a little man. The one who can create can kill. The historian who remembers is frequently the play actor who pretends; the honorable one is sometimes especially tiresome. The ingenious and skillful crafts-

[4] *Op. cit.,* p. 13.
[5] *Notes from Underground,* p. 150.
[6] Goethe, *Hermann and Dorothea, The German Classics,* ed. Francke (New York: The German Publication Society, 1913), I, 57.

man is in the same body also the plunderer; and that one who longs and desires is also the idle, lazy one; while man the wise is simultaneously man the foolish one—and eventually, everywhere, *homo-erector,* the upright one, becomes *homo-crepitans,* the creaking, rattling one, if he lives. Meantime he can so easily become man the *dead one.* If a germ bites, if a gland like a peanut withers, if a valve closes; or if he is punctured or jolted; if he misjudges time, space, or speed; if he eats too much or too little, or waits long enough between breaths, he *dies,* we call it, and begins to turn to mineral. Yet he lives like a god, and his deepest grief, desire, agony, is that he cannot be God. He lives in a mighty contradiction! And the chaos we decry lives within us.

Faith has to face it! The problem of the contradiction has its place in all fields of inquiry and endeavor. The contradiction appears everywhere: in theology as *depravity,* in history as *cruelty* and *wickedness,* in religion as *sin,* in ethics as *evil,* in philosophy as the *problem of the origin and existence of evil,* in psychology as *egocentricity,* and in life itself as *waste of personality*. The problem is everywhere. Was it not Bernard Iddings Bell who said, "Our disorders are not those of mere housekeeping; it is the whole sewer system that is out of whack."

UNIVERSAL HABITAT

Anyone who stumbles around backstage, away from the glitter and painted scenery out front, knows that this evil is everywhere, all around us and as far behind us as the race can remember. It was already an *old* story in the Peloponnesian War when then Athenian envoys spoke to the Melians:

49

The powerful exact what they can, and the weak grant what they must. . . . Of the gods we believe, and of man we know, that by a law of their nature wherever they can rule they will. This law was not made by us, and we are not the first who have acted on it; we did but inherit it, and shall bequeath it to all time, and we know that you and all mankind, if you were as strong as we are, would do as we do.[7]

History knows so little of anything else but evil. Herodotus' *Persian Wars,* Josephus' *Wars of the Jews;* "foolish history," someone says, "knows so little that were not as well unknown": Attila invasions, Children's crusades, Sicilian vespers, Huguenot exiles, Hundred years' wars; "not work but hindrance of work." [8]

The same crimes are committed in Chicago and Cairo, London and Louisville, on the same day; minorities fight everywhere for *Lebensraum;* caste systems of economics and blood, mass graves, and racial debauch do not relieve the hell in the heart of Asia and Africa. During the ninth and tenth centuries gray wolves out of central Europe and Asia virtually took over the kingdom of France. No man could travel at night alone; all carried torches and weapons. But even so, great gray wolves pulled men from their horses and brought them crashing to earth, throat-slit, along the roads. Now it is so with evil. It can be found on most any twenty feet of street the world around.

"O poor mortals," cries Carlyle in *The French Revolution,*

[7] Thucydides, *History of the Peloponnesian War,* Bk. V, p. 105, in *The Greek Historians,* ed. of R. B. Godolphin (New York: Random House, 1942), I, 847.

[8] Thomas Carlyle, *The French Revolution* (Modern Library ed.; New York: Random House), p. 23.

"how ye make this earth bitter for each other." And tell me,
if you can, when has the human heart not been like a
runaway horse? All are involved—everywhere. "All human
life is involved in the sin of seeking security at the expense
of other life." [9] In the warp and woof of this world evil
has a universal habitat. Disease, suffering, pain, evil, are
innate, says Thomas Mann in introducing Dostoevsky's *Short
Novels.* Lin Yutang could not believe an "automatic millennium" would ever blossom in our spiritual desert; he
smelled "too many corpses around." Goethe carries it back
into *Iphigenia,*

> Thus the sons of Tantalus, with
> barbarous hands, have sown curse
> upon curse;
> and, as the shaken weed
> scatters around a thousand poison seeds.

If the matter of responsibility rears its head at this point,
perhaps Lady Anne to Richard Gloucester says it for us all,

> For thou hast made the happy earth thy hell,
> Fill'd it with cursing cries and deep exlaims.
> If thou delight to view thy heinous deeds,
> Behold this pattern of thy butcheries.

As for us, the "white man's mission" has become a taunt instead of a rallying cry for good works. Lin Yutang says it is
a "boomerang." We should have given the Asiatic the Bible,
"which [the White Man] had no use for," and kept the guns

---

[9] Reinhold Niebuhr, *The Nature and Destiny of Man,* Vol. I, *Human
Nature* (New York: Chas. Scribner's Sons, 1941), p. 182.

we use so expertly. Heine said the future smelled like Russian leather to him—with blood, godlessness, and many whippings. He advised his grandchildren to develop very thick skin for their backs. "I do not know," he wrote, "but I think that eventually the great Sea Serpent will have its head crushed and the skin of the Northern Bear will be pulled over its ears. There may be only one shepherd—one flock, one free shepherd with an iron staff, and a shorn-alike, bleating alike human herd." [10]

As for us, the focus of infection that once was Europe is now scattered throughout the body politic, and other gray walls than the Kremlin's have heard the hiss of beginning purges. The bloody dead in Act I of this modern drama weigh heavily at the bottom of the stacks of dead that forty years of reeling down the corridors with knives in our hands have left along the way. For evil, like Lenin, has never concerned itself with the "Kantian, priestly, and vegetarian Quaker prattle about the sacredness of human life."

As for us, it means that the evil everywhere involves us, even when we are momentarily diverted by nicer and more genteel concerns. The tragic drama still goes toward its climax; the denouement, on and off stage, is proceeding. Imperialism is done for, yes, but so is cultural isolationism; so are economic paternalism, racial superiority, and our Western monopoly of life's good things. Too many Easterners have been West to school now; they know the cultural base of the West has its roots in the East, and Asia is claiming her heritage. She writhes and turns in her agony, Africa with her, and there are vassal elements in the West, impatient too.

[10] *Works of Prose.*

The lines are being drawn more clearly for the coming struggle between debtor West and creditor East.[11] History everywhere says it is not likely we shall learn in time to avoid the storm.

> We shall be winnow'd with so rough a wind
> That even our corn shall seem as light as chaff
> And good from bad find no partition.[12]

For evil has a universal habitat, in each and in all, and our gospels preached so patently do not deal with corporate evil.

PROGNOSIS OF EVIL

Indeed, how can our gospels deal with corporate evil before we understand the nature of the malady in its single appearance? Who can prescribe for epidemic who knows no history of a single case? Prognosis must begin in symptomatology with *symptosis,* the emaciation of a single part. We cannot deal with the general aspect of evil until we trace through its particular aspects the course of evil in the single man. Though we *are* in epidemic, the roots of the trouble are still local. Evil is everywhere, but the maggot is in individual brains first.

The Level of Reform

Where evil is recognized as personal, the self-centered man engages in certain man-centered efforts to be rid of his evil. He will admit his faults, submit to being blamed for them,

---

[11] The printed speeches of Charles Malik before the United Nations General Assembly and the World Council of Churches, Evanston, Illinois.

[12] Mowbray in Shakespeare's *King Henry IV,* Act IV, scene 1.

pay for them, even suffer for them. Goethe pointedly adds, "He becomes impatient only if he is required to give them up." At this stage he will even make religious vows about his sins provided the vows are not too costly. "The Hindoos of the desert make a solemn vow to eat no fish." He goes still further in the "religious" approach to his evil, thinks even of reform—as Poins advised young Hal, he "repent[s] at idle times" according as he can. He now comes forward ungrudgingly to support causes, institutions, good works, and other community "props of virtue." He learns the forms of religious respectability yet is much closer to Richard III:

> But then I sigh, and, with a piece of scripture,
> Tell them that God bids us do good for evil:
> And thus I clothe my naked villany
> With old odd ends stolen forth of holy writ,
> And seem a saint when most I play the devil.

And at this stage of evil the self-centered man will even occasionally attempt, honestly and sincerely, to be a good man. He *tries* to be moral. But that is most discouraging to him, for at this level morals mean a "reduction of nature's temperature"; virtue means to want not very much and that without passion;[13] goodness means to stay at home nights; salvation is a kind of bloodletting that keeps the blood pressure and vitality at the freezing point—and he cannot do it! He finds in his own wild nature a very powerful and violent antagonist. He cannot make it—evil is powerful, morals are weak, and salvation is "tallow-faced, with the tips of its

---

[13] Nietzsche: "What good is my virtue? It hath not brought me passion!"

fingers together." He cannot climb out and become a *good* man.

> 'Tis seldom when the bee doth leave her comb
> In the dead carrion.

The Level of Anxiety

When a man knows that he of himself cannot be moral, suspects that he is so centered he cannot escape himself and his sins, here, at the point that he first knows he cannot be more than he is, comes the critical moment. Usually it is here that the tree falls one way or the other. Here he seeks a new center or goes forward into the vale of anxiety, the façade to the theater of overt sinfulness. He becomes anxious about himself and his inabilities; he borders on despair; he refuses to be himself to himself; he begins to learn to dislike himself; he finds he cannot forgive himself either for not becoming what he wants to be or for wanting to be what he is not. Anxiety borders despair; fear edges on trembling. He is concerned, occasionally even agitated, about himself. He checks his symptoms, he is ill, then well; he does not care, but it comes back in the dark and he does care. Unwilling to be himself, unable to be any other self, having only himself to stand upon and around, he evades himself, berates himself, punishes himself, does everything but accept the self in which action alone his salvation from himself could begin. Anxiety edges over into despair; "there is no other self for me to be," he discovers; despair does its secret work; surrender begins; and sooner or later, like the captured Coleville in Henry IV, he gives himself away for nothing, with no bumbling Falstaff to remind him that

"Thou, like a kind fellow, gavest thyself away gratis."
There is, then, left nothing but the progression of evil that
follows surrender.

The Level of Despair

It proceeds with the fading of the thought of any help
from outside himself. The self is too strong for him. He has
heard of God, but he has heard also of self and cannot trust
another. In particular can he not trust any "other" who would
require "all."

> For, though I knew His love Who follow'd,
>   Yet I was sore adread
> Lest, having Him, I must have naught beside.

The truth is unpalatable. Because of unpalatable truth, dread
of himself, the pressure of other concerns and cares, the possibility of reliance on a self outside himself disappears.
Ruskin describes it:

[I had] . . . a continual perception of Sanctity in the whole
of nature, from the slightest thing to the vastest . . . a sort of
heart-hunger, satisfied with the presence of a Great and Holy
Spirit. These feelings remained in their fullest intensity till
eighteen or twenty, and then, as the reflective and practical power
increased, and the "cares of this world" . . . gained upon me,
faded gradually away. . . .[14]

Here one does not bother much to think of sin any more:
to concern oneself with one's own sin is depressing; to think
of the sins of others is unnecessary and presumptuous anyhow.

[14] *Modern Painters.*

Under all this lies that basic and fundamental dissatisfaction with the self—so near to Kierkegaard's despair. The self refuses to be itself before God. The self must be escaped or evaded, and the only available method of escape is the lie that opens the door to sensuality, waste, and a more confirmed self-centeredness. For long he has been unable to live without deceit and lying to the world outside. Now he comes to that level of self-rejection where he does not know that he can no longer tell the truth *within*. He lies to himself, and with the life of lying to himself about himself goes also the business of losing all respect for all others. The only self he knows, trusts, or needs is a lie; hence he ceases to love all selves, including himself. He now substitutes diversity for unity, and for integrity he substitutes activity. There is nothing to hold him from the coarser pleasures and passions that bring men to the borders of bestiality. He commits the "oldest sins the newest kind of ways" and does not know he "strew'st sugar on that bottled spider."

The Level of Sensuality

That is to say, he is becoming what we ordinarily call a thoroughly sensual man. But sensuality is a grossly misused term. Only in its most shallow forms does sensuality involve the tactile senses; only on the narrowest of behavior-pattern levels can sensuality be gauged by appetite for food, sex, and entertainment. Sensuality is no synonym for sexuality, no polite term for lustfulness. Only rarely is the lustful man a sensual man. Most of the time the roué, the libertine, from the standpoint of sexual promiscuity is the most completely spiritual man in sight. He is unfilled spirit, hungry spirit, true

57

enough, but his use of the "senses" is an attempt to satisfy the spirit. The sensual man is the very opposite. He uses the spirit to satisfy the senses; he may be far removed from lust or gourmetish indulgence.

The sensual man is trying to *escape* the self, the lustful man is trying to *find* the self, and there is a difference. The sensual man may be reserved, removed, dignified, sedate, cultured, learned, and respected. His excesses are not often visible, for just as sensuality is no synonym for lustfulness, so it is not always marked by *excesses*.

What makes a sensual man sensual is a spiritual matter, always. It is the net result of the attempt to escape or evade the self by finding another point of reference outside the self. The spirit of the sensual man has tried to escape the consequences of his own spiritual nature. It is the logical consequence of the refusal to be the self. The spirit finds a new god in the processes of bodily existence. It is an attempt to escape selfhood by crawling back into the self. Like Harry in T. S. Eliot's *Family Reunion,* who suddenly learns that "all my life has been a flight," one seeks "to creep back through the little door." [15] It is the question of that nobly sensual man Nicodemus, "How can a man be born when he is old?" How can a man escape the consequences of freedom, responsibility, and other aspects of selfhood? How can he regain the womb where the self is no conscious problem to the self?

[15] *Family Reunion,* Part II, Scene 2; Part I, Scene 1. Used by permission of Harcourt Brace & Co., Inc.

Sensuality is not lust, or excess, or even self-love. It is a perversion of self-love that finds its new god in limitless devotion to purely finite ends. It is a new sense of value: process over existence; present over future; subconscious over the confusions of consciousness; finite over infinite, flesh over spirit. That is to say, to be sensual is to choose the here and the now over everything else; to prefer the demonstrable, weighable, provable, to the leap of faith; to cling to the efficient over the personal; to promote the process above the end. In short, sensuality is scientific in method, logically positivistic or optimistically humanistic or pessimistically naturalistic in philosophy, behavioristic in psychology, and culturally anthropological in religion. Only in his recreation is the sensual man an Epicurean. Niebuhr says it more succinctly when he says,

Sensuality represents an effort to escape from the freedom of the infinite possibilities of the spirit by becoming lost in the detailed processes, activities, and interests of existence, an effort which results inevitably in unlimited devotion to limited values.[16]

The Level of Revenge

The effort to escape into subconscious existence by sensual means, regardless of the degree of self-centeredness and the change of value judgments involved, is ultimately unsuccessful. The outcome of sensualism's failure is revenge on life, "the sweetest morsel to the mouth that ever was cooked in hell." [17] But the true object of revenge is life itself only on

[16] *Op. cit.,* p. 185.

the surface; the revenge is really directed against the unbearable self. Here a man tears at himself like one in a hysteria of pain, like a caught fox gnaws at that part of himself squeezed in the jaws of a trap. Dostoevsky seems to have understood this level of personal evil best. His *Notes from Underground,* his *Crime and Punishment,* are filled with foreboding expressions of that tearing revenge left by sensualism's failure. The diary recorded in the *Notes* is starkly realistic in its disordered progression into the symptosis of personal evil.

I got to the point of feeling a sort of secret abnormal despicable enjoyment in returning home to my corner on some disgusting Petersburg night, acutely conscious that that day I had committed a loathsome action again, that what was done could never be undone, and secretly, inwardly gnawing, gnawing at myself for it, tearing and consuming myself till at last the bitterness turned into a sort of shameful accursed sweetness, and at last—into positive, real enjoyment! . . .

The enjoyment was just from the too intense consciousness of one's own degradation; it was from feeling oneself that one had reached the last barrier, that it was horrible, but that it could not be otherwise; that there was no escape for you; that you never could become a different man; that even if time and faith were still left to you to change into something different you would most likely not wish to change; or if you did wish to, even then you would do nothing; because perhaps in reality there was nothing for you to change into.

. . . .

[17] Credited to Sir Walter Scott.

Now, I am living out my life in my corner, taunting myself
with the spiteful and useless consolation that an intelligent man
cannot become anything seriously, and it is only the fool who
becomes anything.[18]

The Level of Waste

The remnant is waste—utterly useless vestiges of personality, lingering for a miserable moment before sliding
over into the abyss of meaninglessness, nonbeing. It is the
waste Jesus saw burning in Jerusalem at the dump called
Gehenna. Waste is the most awful fact of human existence
because it destroys the most Godlike thing we know, human
personality.

Whole cultures are founded on waste—cities rest their pon-
derous weight on masses of waste, as a trip along any city
water front will sustain. What an appalling squirrel cage of
confusion distorts the culture founded on waste—and the
personality caught in it. The blackest of all the vistas that
overcome our imagination is that of the wasted human personality, a greater multitude than all the savages of Africa and
the sealands, who in "Christian" cities have lived and known
little else than to be causes and victims of the waste of personal evil. This is the waste that leaves the remnant of a man
as Heine saw him:

> I saw thee in a dream. Oh, piteous sight!
> I saw thy heart all empty, all in night;
> I saw the serpent gnawing at thy heart;
> I saw how wretched, O my love, thou art!

[18] Pp. 132-33, 130-31. Reprinted from *The Short Novels of Dostoevsky*
edited by Thomas Mann. Copyright 1945 by the Dial Press.

Until, at the last, outraged life takes over and slaps back-handedly to destroy the remnant—and this is the final level of prognosis—in this life it is the end of the matter. Where man is central, he makes a hell that comes at last to an end where a man finds himself like Hall Caine's lamb surrounded by ravens, crows, and owl-eagles. They have pecked out its eyes and now drive it, blind and bleeding, over a precipice so that they can gorge themselves on its broken body.

Or better said, the hell a self-centered man has gone through in the stages of reform, anxiety, surrender, sensuality, revenge, and waste was seen and felt and understood by Oscar Wilde as he demonstrates in his *Ballad of Reading Gaol*:

> And all the woe that moved him so
>   That he gave that bitter cry,
> And the wild regrets, and the bloody sweats,
>   None knew so well as I:
> For he who lives more lives than one
>   More deaths than one must die.
>
> .   .   .   .
>
> *Each narrow cell in which we dwell*
>   *Is a foul and dark latrine,*
> *And the fetid breath of living Death*
>   *Chokes up each grated screen,*
> *And all, but Lust, is turned to dust*
>   *In Humanity's machine.*

MALPRACTICE

In our combat with that evil—corporate and personal—in seeking to live in this world, we men of religion have once

62

more added more burdens than we have removed. Religion has countered evil with weapons that will not work—some of which she bought from the enemy. There is in the record of religion a long history of malpractice.

When the really shocking realization that this is an evil world reaches to the nerve centers of religion, the first inclination is to *run for a refuge;* we seek to withdraw from the encounter. There have been many *stylites* to follow old Simeon, the Elder, of Syria. On their sacred pillars they draw out their lives in mumbling uselessness, separated, above the evil by thirty feet or so. Indeed, when have we been further from evil than that? One of us even stayed above evil for sixty-eight years that way,[19] but it is at best a lonesome way. Most of us, when we run from evil, prefer to run in company with other like-minded sprinters, and swarms of "Holy Cities" have dotted various landscapes. Not even "Reformation" halted the evacuation toward Zion, as the records of the Genevans, Taborites, certain Anabaptists, the new-world movement, the followers of old Jean de Labadie, William Penn, and the Woman in the Wilderness all testify. In more modern times the Paradise Seekers, the Brook Farm people, the Shakers and their woman Christ, the Mormons, and Father Divine's thousands of "Angels" speak as loudly as any. Nor is the exodus done.

The genteel version of this hoary remedy is a virulent one and is perhaps best expressed as our nucleoplasmic way of life in organized religious circles. We try to preserve our holy identity by wrapping an insulating covering around the germ,

---

[19] Simeon the Younger, said to have become a stylite at five years of age, continuing until his death, A.D. 597, near Antioch.

a reticular substance around the nucleus. We will meet evil by withdrawing into isolated and segregated little sacks. So into our wonderful brick and stone (nearly fireproof) new shells we go. No evil must besmirch the Lord's elect!

But can the Church really forget its witness where the Cross and the evil and the people are? When did he ever say that his followers were to become sacrosanct societies for the preservation of ancient human opinions? When did he commission us to be doughty defenders of certain pious patterns? Who called us to become withered recluses of a year dead a millennium behind us? Why would he shut us up to ourselves like monks in a monastery mumbling a mass? Did he really create these sacred sororities for snubbing sinners? It was not intended so to be! Let us come away from this defensive business!

Nor can we base our hopes for dealing with evil on the shifting strata of false statistics that add up to give us our annual illusions of success and the institutional mediocrity that holds "fast-bound the hosts of God." Too much of the apparent strength of the institutionalized church is not strength. As Carlyle insisted, "The first of all gospels is this; that a lie cannot endure forever";[20] and too much of our mass profession is a lie, a fad, a social nicety. In *Pilgrim's Progress,* Pliable still comes out of the slough on the same side he entered. This institutional monstrosity we have named church is too filled with people who nibble at religion. Their vaunted independence in the spiritual house is actually a vicious kind

[20] *Op. cit.,* p. 30

of undependability. Institutionalized mediocrity halters the church until we stand, like dumb oxen, lowing for provender of tithes, goaded nicely by the timid tenders we hire for our pulpit stalls, inanimate, numerically and superficially "growing," bound in old odd harness straps, covered with the graveclothes of our past, dragging a cargo of old wineskins full of tradition and dogma, with our herd-back turned to the common facts of life like prejudiced segregation, vicious business, soulless education, and rote, colorless religion.

There are other remedies that will not work. Ignore evil, perhaps he will go away; deny evil, perhaps he is not really there; invite him in, who knows but that he could be tamed? involve him in a conversation, perchance we can confuse him with our high-sounding terms. In other words we have tried to answer evil with four minor and most inane home remedies; activism, mere belief, petty morals, and pseudo intellectualisms.

"O day of rest and gladness," we sometimes sing on Sundays. Not so! To a life already cluttered enough is added on Sunday another day of fussy-minded busyness: societies, committees, boards, groups, meetings, programs. The idea of the remedy of activism is to bury your doubts, longings, and particularly your questions under a multitude of pious activities. We must play hard in order to be able to forget we live in a haunted house. "Play many fast games, children, and the serpents in the garden will be so disturbed by your obvious 'pleasure in the work' that they will leave us to ourselves." Ignore evil, perhaps he will go away, if we are very very busy. "Whirl is King" even in church, but the only gain for us so far has been the greater capacity for a variety of sensations. Religion cannot be a function we perform at stated times, on Sundays and Wednesdays, perhaps. It has something to do with Monday mornings and Saturday afternoons. One does not get away from God or from evil by going to or staying away from the merry-go-round at church.

"Only believe," nothing is impossible; "only believe," by which we have meant believing the unbelievable. Protect your naïve acceptance of the unthinkable as a little boy protects his Sunday-school penny from the big boys on the corner by clenching it tightly in a grubby little hand. But there is no redemption, even from ignorance, much less evil, in the belief of anyone's *list of believables*. Redemption from the evil is an affair between persons, and mere belief cannot do it. How silly of us to deny evil in the hope that he is not really there. There is no saving encounter in "belief about," for even the demons "believe and tremble." There is no validity anywhere now in the promotion of cluttered ignorance in the name of a religion that fears truth like it fears the devil and rejects man's right to question and deny and doubt. That kind of belief in that sort of religion can issue only where one has said we could be coming out: in a "frivolous disregard of moral questions . . . ; a confusion of values; a blurring of moral distinctions; a lack of principle . . . ; and acquiescence in the meaninglessness of life." [21]

"All in our places, with bright shining faces," will hardly

[21] Ralph Barton Perry, *Puritanism and Democracy* (New York: The Vanguard Press, 1944), p. 628.

do it either. The burden of regimented petty morals is an onerous and limping answer to the threat of the serpent—really not quite adequate. One of last summer's neighborhood tragedies was the sudden demise of Torchy, a peace-loving cocker spaniel who innocently tangled with a venom-swollen copperhead somewhere in Tarrytown's shrubbery. Our neighbor, the red-haired son of the Presbyterian manse nearby, turned out to deal with that vicious reptile, barefoot and armed with a water pistol! Quite fortunately, he did not find it. Nor does our expedition of regimented petty morals, barefoot and carrying its water gun, ever come to grips with evil. Somehow the two pass each other in the shadows. Nor is it likely that evil knows we passed. Not even moralism's bigger brother, legalism, can help us much. Law knows the right, but not the good; it knows justice, but not life itself. The law suppresses, but "it merely drives that chaos inward and does not conquer or regenerate it" [22] Law produces a morality of the herd, but it cannot lift one above the herd to victory over self, evil, and into the personal and individual. Legal righteousness becomes damnable righteousness and is condemned even by evil. Lawful goodness is flat goodness, dull goodness. "How strange to find so little good in goodness," says Gogol. Legalism lets the "righteous fight their way into Paradise over the corpses of their neighbors." [23] The answer to evil of lowered vitality, suppressed individuality, the goodness of inactivity, the virtue

[22] Nicolas Berdyaev, *The Destiny of Man*, tr. Natalie Duddington (New York: Chas. Scribner's Sons, 1937), p. 116. Used by permission of Geoffrey Bles Ltd.

[23] *Ibid.*, p. 147.

of wanting little, the lowered temperature of lackadaisical and surrendered nature, is no answer for wild evil. It only keeps the serf "in his place," and once made him submit to "Seigneur," who could, as he returned from hunting, "kill not more than two serfs, and refresh his feet in their warm blood and bowels." [24] The law does nothing for persons— and so cannot deal with evil any better than its little brother, petty moralism, though law carries a bigger gun. Moralism indeed invites evil into the house, but cannot tame him.

If evil cannot be ignored, denied, or tamed, there is one more drug untried in our medicine chest. Let us *confuse* him; let us befuddle him with definitions and technical terms, split-hair distinctions and varicose mental meanderings down the corridors of intellectual mazes he cannot follow. Let us teach our young theologues the jargon of psycho-therapy; condition them to analyze, like proper young Neo-Freudians, every human notion and emotion; equip them with "techniques" of group counseling; teach them Latin names for all normal manifestations of sick or sinful personality. Let us atomize evil by sending out one-eyed technicians with fine cures for old ailments, therapists with pink-pill mottoes about "living positively." Organize us into colonies with culture, background, cosmopolitan manners, prayer calendars, and foam mattresses in every retreat cell, along with Persian carpets on every floor and a divine healer under every bed. Crowning our thrust against evil with these pseudo intellectualisms, these therapies of crass materialism,

[24] Carlyle, *op. cit.,* p. 11.

we will develop queen bees of the devotional hive to teach us how to retreat from life, mouth our modern panaceas, and contribute to the upkeep of the castellated Victorian mansions that house the "new approach" and print such beautiful slick brochures and breed these "divinely different" accents to dazzle us ordinary sinners with the vocabulary of the holiness that overcomes nothing but boredom for those whom it calls apart. Satan must be terrified at the threat!

Give to any man a full measure of all these answers to evil. Let him have all he can hold of activism, mere belief, morals, and the "new look"; then

shower upon him every earthly blessing, drown him in a sea of happiness, so that nothing but bubbles of bliss can be seen on the surface; give him economic prosperity, such that he should have nothing else to do but sleep, eat cakes and busy himself with the continuation of his species, and even then out of sheer ingratitude, sheer spite, [he] would play you some nasty trick.[25]

The problem of evil is not so simply met. There is more to it than these lame answers can carry. They are like the balloon designed for the defenses of Paris which "mounted heavenward, so beautifully, so unguidably." During the revolution one citizen worked out the scheme of a huge wooden cannon "which France shall exclusively profit by." It was to be made of staves by the coopers of Paris. Thomas Carlyle reports that the wooden cannon was "of almost boundless calibre, but uncertain as to strength."[26] There must be a better cure!

[25] Dostoevsky, *Notes from Underground*, p. 149.
[26] *Op. cit.*, p. 481.

THE CHRISTIAN SPECIFIC

A "specific" for evil? How bold can you get? There is surely no mysterious prescription pad marked Rx that a man may wave at evil. To imagine it smacks of superstition and to proclaim it would be primitively animistic, if not a fetishism.

The Christian runs the risk of that accusation. He is as bold about evil as the Christian faith itself. We know this world is evil; we do not try to evade it; we know we are hemmed in on every hand, cut off, frustrated, bound; but we are not "timid souls" withal. There is a holy boldness about us in the face of evil:

"We are troubled on every side, yet not distressed; we are perplexed, but not in despair; persecuted, but not forsaken; cast down, but not destroyed; . . ."

(II Cor. 4:8-9.)

And all this is ours because "we have this treasure." The Christian understands Luther correctly when he says "sin boldly," not that "grace may abound," but because he knows he can never escape it all; it is all around him, in him, he is continually engaged, but he is bold about it—he neither runs, nor hides, nor despairs. He has the specific—Rx—which is first of all—

The Person

Men have known nearly always that the answer to so personal a power as evil is a Person. It is a bona fide expression of that "other" side of the mighty contradiction within him that man will not give up the *search for the Person*. The

70

false answers and persons at which we have arrived have not turned us away from the prospect of a religious answer to evil and our search for Person. "Men hate and despise religion, but they are afraid it may be true," [27] or, at least, afraid that there may be truth hidden somewhere within its symbols and mysteries. So the search continues for a religious and valid answer—"so great a thing that it is only fair that those who will not take the trouble to seek it should be forced to go without it." [28]

This longing search for the good is the search for God. The search for God is the search for a Person, and it springs from the fact, says Berdyaev, "that we cannot bear to be faced forever with the distinction between good and evil and the bitterness of choice." [29]

For what kind of Person must we search? If the cause of all the chaos and disintegration in this world is that there are as many centers of the universe as there are human beings, then the answer to all the chaos and disintegration will begin in that Person who is fit to become the center for all the universes we single men inhabit. That is to say, we search for that One who is able to occupy the throne at the center of all men's lives everywhere. And the Christian faith teaches that that One is here and has been searching for us as well. This is the One that Christian faith puts on the throne of history. We make no bones about it! We set the One who knew that he was Son of God at history's center, at time's center, on a throne. And in our faith in a *personal* Messiah we

[27] Pascal, *Pensées* (New York: The Modern Library, 1941).
[28] *Ibid.*
[29] *Op. cit.,* p. 21.

71

see the highest development of the truth that the only saving element history has ever known has been *personal*—that is, salvation has always involved the appearance of persons able to save. The Christian faith puts Christ on history's throne and claims that the only union possible to mankind occurs only when he is our Center, Lord, and Master.

In recent decades there has appeared a rather widespread acceptance of the old claim that the "idea" of God is a projection, from Feuerbach, Freud, and others. H. Wheeler Robinson asks, "Is it only a projection?" [30] while quoting W. R. Matthews—"Does the projection hit anything?" [31] Projection or no, both accuser and defender have to deal with the fact and person of Jesus Christ, who makes either the projection of God as idea or the truth of God as fact come alive. He is alive, regardless, to the Christian faith. He is the Person upon whom the center descends. The faith is not the Christian faith whenever it evades, resists, or denies the Person at the center. Christianity is not a "statutory" religion. The morphology of Christianity is a changing complex; none of its "forms" are eternally valid save the center alone. Its gospel and its faith exist, and must exist, as Adolf Harnack has said, "under most diverse conditions. . . . if it is to be the religion of the living and is itself to live." [32] The Christian essential is the Person, Christ, who has as aim to show the living God as his own to every in-

[30] *Redemption and Revelation in the Actuality of History* (New York: Harper & Bros., 1942), p. 11.

[31] *The Gospel and the Modern Mind* (New York: Geo. H. Doran Co., 1925), p. 90.

[32] *What Is Christianity?* (New York: G. P. Putnam's Sons, 1901), p. 191.

dividual. Christ is to history as the idea of God is to nature. He is even more conceptually real than historically real. He is not ever mere person but embodies a whole way of seeing the universe of God and man and our mutual relations.[33] He is Christianity, and the God he reveals as center is anxious to draw us unto himself as the answer to evil.

"Why is God landing in this enemy-occupied world in disguise?" asks C. S. Lewis. "Why isn't he landing in force, invading it?" [34] Lewis' answer—"When the author walks onto the stage the play's over"—is not his full answer. The Author has come "onstage," and the play is not over. God has entered into our experience, and as always there is "something we can understand and something that passes understanding." [35] It is he, the Faith declares, who has so powerfully entered history that history is redemptive history; in all its sweeping and turnings the Redeemer is at work. Which brings us to the second element of the Christian specific: The Person is involved in a series of events called by the Scriptures "mighty acts."

The Event

The goal of history according to the Christian faith is the realization of its center. This is the salvation of the world, that all men find that Person at the center. He is at history's center from the very beginning, claims John and the writer of the letter to Jewish Christians. And then, in recognition of a poignant paradox Hebrews takes cognizance of the state of

[33] See Fairbairn, *op. cit.,* pp. 16 ff.

[34] *The Case for Christianity* (New York: The Macmillan Co., 1943), pp. 55-56.

[35] Robinson, *op. cit.,* p. 16.

things in this conflict-ridden present by adding, *"We see not yet all things put under him, but we see Jesus . . ."* (2:8*b*-9*a*), the Person, the beginning of that series of "mighty acts" which constitute Event.

That is to say, event is *advent.* He became a man, "made a little lower than the angels. . . . He also himself likewise took part of the same [flesh and blood]. . . . He took not on him the nature of angels; but he took on him the seed of Abraham . . . like unto his brethren . . ."; he became a man! The event begins in the advent of the Word which was made flesh, "made in the likeness of men." Event is incarnation, which means of itself an interruption whether the world knows it or not. And here person, the quality of personalness, once more presses to the foreground. He identifies himself with human personalness in the same interrupting way that characterizes all incarnation. All birth of personality is incarnation. If this were not true, man would be like anything else; nothing unusual would mark him.[36] But this is the basis of our kinship with this Person:

> When a person enters the world, a unique and unrepeatable personality, then the world process is broken into and compelled to change its course, in spite of the fact that outwardly there is no sign of this. . . . The existence of personality presupposes interruption. . . . Personality is a break through, a breaking in upon this world; it is the introduction of something new.[37]

A person is unique, of another origin, a microcosm, capable

---

[36] See Berdyaev on "Personality" in *Slavery and Freedom* (New York: Chas. Scribner's Sons, 1944), pp. 20-59.

[37] *Ibid.,* p. 21.

of entrance into infinity; he is individually unrepeatable, always subject, never object; he is a category of value, a primary whole, indestructible, an irreplaceable form, as Gestalt psychology knows. And it is just this that the Person at the center of history assumes in the advent. He became a man. But there is more.

He became a man involved, caught, in predicament; he is existential man. And here appears the border line between event and drama. His becoming man, involved, results in decision, action, deed, drama. And the deed?

It is primarily Cross. But the Cross is everywhere; all incarnated men know Cross. It is written into life. So back again to Person. The significance of this particular Cross is dependent upon the identity of this particular person involved in Cross. The validity of the deed lies wholly on the uniqueness of the Person.

The genius of the Christian "specific" for evil appears in the identity of the Person. Incarnation is only the means of involving the Person in event which issues in Cross-Drama. The identity is the thing. Who is he? The faith says he is *monogenes,* the only one of his kind. The faith says he is God, involved, caught, in encounter, suffering himself the agony of the mighty contradiction. This changes things. For if God is not *ultra pura,* absolute; if instead he is present, engaged, involved, en route, so to speak—if he really comes to us—then in what sense is the Cross reconciliation? His coming is evidence he does not need to be reconciled. In what sense is the Cross vicarious? Our suffering is evidence that it is not. In what sense is his death substitutionary, a ransom,

75

or a juridical satisfaction? There must be more. As indeed there is, much more.

The event is atonement, a much-abused word desperately in need of rescue from its users. There is little, if any, validity left in the common notion of the Cross as ransom, substitution, or satisfaction. I cannot longer preach it so and have been driven myself upon the cross that wrenches out a *vital view*. What is this vital view of atonement?

Any valid doctrine of redemption must take into account a deeper view of sin-evil and a wider view of salvation from evil than more orthodox frames of reference can permit. Any valid view of sin must take into account the depth of human personality, must consider what we now know of the nature of human beings, must begin with man as he is, where he is—involved in a *Gestalt,* a form irreplaceable, plunging into the depths or arising out of the depths of nonbeing, chaos, cross, if you please. That is to say, a true view of the Cross will not attempt by substitution, ransom, or any other means to *disengage man from his own being and the Gestalt of cross that shapes his being*. The atonement must involve the *self-as-it-is* and God-as-he-is.

The vital view of the Cross-deed sees this redemption-event as both *ultimate identification* and *ultimate denial of identification*. At the Cross the self owns the self and refuses to remain the self. The self admits itself and gives itself away, and in this are involved both the identification of the self with evil and the identification of the self with God. At the Cross, Christ is supremely Man-God, and at the Cross man is forced to deny first his Godhood by admitting his selfhood and to deny his selfhood by receiving his Godhood. In denying himself he is lifted out of himself. Only the legalist denies himself something. The Cross is the denial of self—and Jesus on it *shows us how*.

This is the event which issues in redemption. There is no other way than escape from selfness into otherness. The validity of the Cross lies in the presence of a *double ultimate:* the ultimate of selfness, I-ness, id; and the ultimate of otherness, Thou-ness, God. The encounter between them is within the drama that includes the Person, the mighty acts of God in Christ, and all the continuing incarnation-involvement of all the selves who at the Cross are exposed to the loneliness of self—and the loneliness of God when each is left alone in self.

The Drama

The drama is the drama of redemption for all who will become involved, engaged, in encounter at the center of things. At the Cross I must look up, as Paul Scherer says, "into the face of His eternal judgment on my sins, and that eternal mercy for my soul." The Cross is both judgment of self and mercy for self, but not because it is the only Cross, nor even because it is the only Cross God will share; rather, its mercy and judgment lie in the fact that it is the only Cross he inhabits *exclusively*. Someone else is on all the others, even though with him. He does not save me from suffering, nor even from sinning.

Yet the drama of redemption, involving God as actor, Cross as stage, and the encounter between self and God as situation, begins to involve me only at the point of my sur-

77

render—at the edge of the sacrifice of self which introduces me to the redemptive nature of suffering and shatters my selfish heart. It is *only* here that

> . . . he of the swollen purple throat,
>   And the stark and staring eyes,
> Waits for the holy hands that took
>   The Thief to Paradise;
> And a broken and a contrite heart
>   The Lord will not despise.[38]

It is here that any involved man caught in the contradiction can cry, "Hear me, O look up! See how my heart which hath been closed so long, doth open to the bliss of seeing thee!" [39] As a child I was contrite over what I had done; as a man my broken heart is because of what I am; and there, at the point of my desire to lose the self in finding him, there he finds me, he captures me, his cross seizes me:

> Let me no more my comfort draw
>   From my frail hold of Thee,
> In this alone rejoice with awe—
>   Thy mighty grasp of me.[40]

And seizing me, he transforms me; and now begins my exaltation above the evil which surrounds, infills, and wounds from behind. Now I am a Christ-ian. "I have made my response to a great redeeming act and love which constrains

---

[38] Oscar Wilde, *The Ballad of Reading Gaol.*
[39] Goethe, *Iphigenia.*
[40] John Campbell Shairp.

me to be a redemptive person in my sphere, giving myself because One loved me and gave Himself." [41]

Transformation and response are by-products of the drama of redemption, but what is my response? It is the response of *obedience* and *trust*. And the transformation? "Strange," says Luther, "that though I am redeemed from sin, yet am I not redeemed from sinning." And again, *"Semper justus; semper peccator,"* always justified—always sinner. Do I win the contradiction over? Now am I finished with the evil? Not at all, not hardly, and this is the meaning both of my continuing sacrifice of obedience and of the drama itself. The war is won, but the battle is not done.

It is to this essential incompleteness that the Christian must surrender himself. He must even surrender himself to the possibility of his own battle turning out to be a losing battle! His surrender means he is no longer obsessed with what happens to himself. He is willing to be damned for the good of the day's fight, yet for that willingness he must fight even the pride that can inhabit his own redeemed self. He is not done with sinning still—nor has he heard of evil the last time.

Then, have we gone full circle? Is the Christian specific no specific? "We have this treasure" of Person, Event, and Drama, and it is a specific for evil, but the Christian must know that the treasure is "in earthen vessels." There is no solution of the problem of evil short of the full knowledge of God himself, and "what thou knowest is not God!" [42] But we see the victory, and that is something! In the midst

---

[41] Samuel Angus, *Essential Christianity* (New York: The Macmillan Co., 1939).

[42] Augustine.

of the drama in which we are involved we see that his creative action has not ceased, and what we have mistakenly thought to be the Creator's absence for Sabbath rest has become a beneficent, creative activity in our behalf.

We see the collapse of life and morals, whirling change on clouds of death for individual forms, but we have discovered also that mankind has been unable to forget the Cross by which he has gained such an insight into the surrender of life itself which forms the turning point in history's great advances.

We see the end of blood sacrifice when we see the new epoch history marks at that point where love went to death and shows the way through death. For men, here and there at least, have learned that life will do its own sacrificing of the pure, and the just, and the beautiful, in spite of which we rejoice, for to our amazement in every episode of our suffering there issues some redemption to the need around us.

We know that "self is the great negation of God," but we know also that crossroad at which the self may be rid of itself in the power which shaped it. We know we exist before God, but as Kierkegaard confessed, we do not go crazy, nor are we brought to nought, for we have overcome that self that is the "sickness . . . unto death." We know we are "run to a stand still," but where we stop, heaving and shaking, God has always met us.

We know our fellow man, the "ungrateful biped" with his "perpetual moral obliquity," but we also know that it has not been the Christ-man who has soaked the world in tears

80

and blood and has sent whole battalions, bloody and reeling, down the narrow alleyways.

We have not claimed that human nature has changed, but we have seen human beings go through ordeal, cleansing, and grace into new life, and in the new life we see them become redeemer-creators in themselves. We have even tasted the redemption they have released to the need around them. We know the "relativity" of our knowledge, the "perils of belief," and the "abyss of meaninglessness [which] yawns on the brink of all [our] spiritual endeavors," but this does not terrify us, nor does our experience of the way of faith as a life of ups and downs, for we have seen too many "dinosaurs turn into lizards that a man can kick around with his foot."

We know that human history is a wild jungle, "red in tooth and claw," without any real meaning to the unredeemed; but to us, in the light of His Cross and ours, "history is a matrix out of which emerge, in response to the call of God, *men and women who eternally matter,* . . . who . . . live in such a fashion as, if all men lived that way, would make our earth a part of Heaven rather than a vestibule to Hell!" [43]

Outside the walls of Carthage, Benson says in his great life of Cyprian, thousands of dull monuments teach us nothing but names; but within the graves are Christian emblems and beheaded skeletons with their skulls resting upon their laps. And who are these? We do not know; we just know there are less noble kinds of suffering and crucifixion, for did not that Nietzsche whom Papini called the "poor, syphilitic,

[43] Bernard Iddings Bell, *God Is Not Dead* (New York: Harper & Bros., 1945), pp. 28-29.

81

Anti-Christ" sign his last letter "The crucified One"? There are other kinds of crucifixion; we have chosen the higher one, for within the drama of redemption we have learned to look toward an epilogue. The play does not close with us or ours.

The drama continues—the redemption of history itself. Meantime, we win no final victory over evil, but we win victories. We have no final resting place, but we know rest. There is no cessation of the conflict, but we sing songs in the nighttime. Despair does not destroy possibility, even though our own best day against evil brought only a temporary lull in the hostilities. We know also the dark night of the soul in defeat, but not for long, and in spite of the fact that our personal encounters with evil never bring more than "gradational" separation from evil,[44] yet we have a faith—a confident look about us born of the sure word of hope—

> "A faith that frustration will not be
> the final writing."

At the close of every sheet of copy in our lives, including the last, the author puts that word for the typesetter's eye,

"More."

[44] See Tsanoff's great book *The Nature of Evil* (New York: The Macmillan Co., 1931).

82

CHAPTER THREE

FAITH and the FALCON

Next day, before the great log fire in the main lounge, waiting impatiently for the plows to clear the way for our pell-mell rush to confusion, we talked of how narrow the corner and of the Falcon that hovered over us. We were not surprised to find ourselves so opposed, or so involved, for three days of ultimate questioning had inured us to the lack of politeness in our encounters, and we had discovered we were concerned, involved, tormented men who sought answers to identical problems. And you, Victor, with eight languages and years of roving residence as a world citizen, and I, at home in just one mountain valley, were hunting release from the Falcon that held us both in our provincialism.

FAITH AND THE FALCON

From my birth they have hovered over me:
tradition, authority, patterns, rules, and prejudices
I never made, binding me.
Like Nietzsche I have cried
for the home of a free spirit, but the Falcon
that is our culture bides his time.
He can afford to soar there, waiting.
His victim is bound, and in this human situation
we all share the same strictures.
Is there the freedom of release
for Faith in that Eternal Presence
who will not let me lie content in my shackles?

WHEN YOU GROW UP IN THE CUMBERLANDS, you are in the heart of the "purest Anglo-Saxon populace on the face of the earth," they say, everybody you know says. In the Cumberlands, they tell you, there just is no other kind of blood—much. Your Saxon ancestors liked the mountains, and topography, prejudice, and poverty kept it Anglo-Saxon. There are no "foreigners" for you to see. Because the sons of the only Jewish family are your friends, you do not know of anti-Semitism. A very dark white man spoke at your church once and took a collection for the survivors of the Turkish massacres. You had never seen a Turk in all your life and knew they must be a fearful people. This is all very upsetting to you when the city police arrest your "missionary" miles away for soliciting funds in behalf of survivors of an incident that happened twenty-five years before. You had a quarter in that collection! The first Chinaman you ever saw operated a laundry in Bristol, and as a twelve-year-old you follow him three blocks, at a good safe distance.

Without knowing it, you are caught in a cultural stricture, the Anglo-Saxon myth. Your congressman, who comes on the Fourth of July, and the only college president you ever saw until you were twenty both say the same things. You, they tell you, are an Anglo-Saxon; this is nice, because it means you have character, integrity, religion, and courage. Even if you are "slow to take to strangers," no other race is like you, and nothing could be better than to be what you are: a white, Anglo-Saxon, southern, mountain man.

The only Negro people you know are Sam, who helps with barbecues, Jessie, who works at the Presbyterian manse next door, and Jessie's sons, with whom you play. Because these are your friends, they are Anglo-Saxon too, and you all go along to heaven together. Only in occasional rock fights with the Bassel-town small fry do your real prejudices speak out. Otherwise, it is a safe, friendly, wonderful world, Anglo-Saxon world. Years later you look back sometimes and wish it were still there.

At sixteen your world gets bigger, and it becomes apparent that in that Anglo-Saxon world most of its citizens really believe what you have always heard: that white culture, especially the Teutonic, is superior; that other races can never equal yours; that pride of family, ancestor worship, especially

86

the military ones, is good and helps preserve our purity; that some races are especially equipped to be the "hewers of wood and drawers of water" that your prosperity requires, and decay follows any mixing of races.

What did this to you and yours? How did you get that way? Where did you get these old midwives' tales of your supremacy? Then you begin a frantic attempt to understand your culture. You find a pagan dream, a Saxon tradition, a Prussian pride in crusade, an empire and a spirit that spreads: England, America, southern myth of aristocracy, white supremacy, economic vassalage, and a hundred years from the War, there are governors and senators to speak of unequal facilities as if they were equal and as if this fixed everything, and they are saying just what the midwives of racism have always said.

This is how your culture binds you. And at the mention of his prejudice the hair stands on the back of a man's neck like hackles on a fighting hound.

And what is prejudice? It is a vicious kind of mental slant pushed up out of your culture that makes up your mind for you before you think. It is an evil kind of mental blind spot that shuts from your view the facts in a given situation. It is a tyrannous mental fence that holds you from friendships you need and confines you to your own backyard. It may be racial, religious, sectional, economic, or social. It is always personal, and in some sense it is always cultural. It is a symptom of pride, ignorance, and ego anywhere it happens to you, and it cuts across justice, perverts truth, subsists on lies, and worse; it twists and wastes personality, for whose sake culture exists to begin with.

When you know this, then the culture that surrounds you also binds you. Even the strictures of your life itself are no more formidable than your sameness, your shallowness, your smugness, your provincialisms, and your prejudices.

Wherever you are born, they hover over you: tradition, authority, patterns, rules you never made, binding you. Like Nietzsche you cry for the home of a free spirit, but the falcon that is your culture bides his time. He can afford to soar there, waiting. His victim is bound, and in this human situation you share your strictures with all you meet.

So you look for escape. Is there the freedom of release in that faith which will not let me lie content in my shackles?

But even that faith, the Christian faith, has had to face the same problem and fight its way out of a culture that has never been able to hold it.

THE FERMENT OF HISTORY

Indeed, the faith was born in a receptacle too small to hold it. Its first great victory was its triumph over the receptacle of its origin, for to be Jewish in that world, and a sect of Judaism at that, was a fatal malady for a new religion. But the faith grew beyond this barrier, and so well that in World War II an old lady in Europe decried Hitler's base charges for she was quite sure Jesus had been a Pole and not a Jew.

What an enemy the sprawling Roman Empire must have seemed to the insignificant Jewish sect. Perhaps they did not know they had to conquer *that!* And so they took advantage of Roman *les majestie* to grow from their pitiable five hundred to such "multitudes of men," says Tertullian, in that first 180 years that their removal would "cover the empire with shame." [1] Then, too, perhaps they did know—and welcomed the wild incursions of another potential enemy, the dread men of the North and West. At any rate, as so often since, history seemed to conspire with force and with disaster in favor of faith, until Attila. And then?

Not even the current movie makers know what Leo said to Attila outside Rome that day, but it was enough, and the superstitious Hun turned back with his near million men on a trail he had followed fourteen years, leaving the faith in a strong institutional frame well placed on top of the rotting heap Rome had become. Subsequent incursions did not dislodge it.

Meanwhile, faith was involved in more than six centuries of the agony and conflict of theological definition. Who is Jesus? From whence does he come? What is his nature? Of what stuff is he made, or was he made? What does the faith mean by "triune God"? Does the Holy Spirit issue in series from Son and Father, or like the Son, is he an independent issue? Old Arius fell over in offal and died, [2] a judgment of God, they said, but his ideas are alive across eighteen centuries while Pelagius and Augustine can still provoke bitter in-faculty cleavages. But that first six centuries? Brutal they were—and the new faith threatened to fly apart at the seams of its thought, yet it did not.

Not even the so-called "threat of darkness" and the so-called "collapse" of the Middle Ages could do it. The Mohammedan

---

[1] *Apologeticus,* XXXVII.

[2] Socrates, *Ecclesiastical History,* I, XXXVIII, p. 78 (London: Henry G. Bohn, 1853); and Sozomen, H. E., *Ecclesiastical History* (London: Henry G. Bohn, 1855), II, XXIX; XXX (the account of Athanasius), pp. 98-99.

hammer rammed across North Africa, crossed at Gibraltar, and thrust itself up against another kind of hammer, the steel-clad Goths of Tours and Poitiers—then circled, reforged its head, and rattled the hinges on Maximilian's palace nearly a millennium later. But Saladin could not do it either, and the hammer was not to strike out of Asia again until time for Winston Churchill to say during the Berlin lift, "they never came back—till now!"

The faith was not secure—it never has been—but it was not because of the collapse of the old as much as it was the rise, the whirling, maddening rise, of the new. There has not appeared, until now, a wilder, more fruitful time. New ideas about *everything;* universities, scholasticism, fruitless crusades, the recovery of Greek thought, Saracen skills, Saracen customs, Saracen wisdom, feudalism, vandalism, all bombarded these pagan Christian peoples of the thirteenth century. Amazing superstition in theology, amazing ignorance in science, amazing impiety in religion, flowered into a day when priests actually despoiled their own altar cloths with human excrement in some of the churches of Paris, and a St. Stephen's Day Mass featured a poem sung to the ass. In this whelping, brawling, powerful, maddening maze not even institutional rigidity could choke out that gospel which now stood on the lip of a great shift to the modern culture that so constricts us. It was not decay but ferment, and out of *ferment* came something new.

THE CULTURE THAT BINDS US

That world of the mid-fifteenth century hardly knew it, but out of the agony behind had appeared a new set of problems. Those problems and the subsequent answer to the problems gave our modern culture its current sources.

Ideas and Men

This culture first saw the new day in terms of a new definition of an old acquaintance—the universe. This is the key to the new. After A.D. 1470 men could no longer accept the fact that the familiar is known; from here on out the known must be questioned and known again to be known. When Socrates approached death, he asked Crito to sacrifice a rooster early in the morning to express his gratitude at his release from "terrible life." As for us, this terrible life began to happen the day Copernicus first began to say, "The earth is not the center of things." On this terrible idea our security began to shatter, and it need not have been. But the theologians at Padua had no heart for looking at the moon through Galilei's telescope. "We might see that we cannot believe." So, fumbling back and forth between his faith, which he wished to keep, and his new knowledge, which he could not relinquish, Galileo Galilei died, and the new age waited for Newton. The story was different when Newton died. The universe, men knew, no longer ran by the arbitrary will of God; it was a law-governed unity. Copernicus, Galilei, Kepler, and Newton had said the earth is not the center, and the procession was just beginning.

On the heels of the dread new universe came a *new technique,* inductive logic. Bacon insisted that truth could no longer be deduced from religious authority; rather, it must be arrived at inductively on the basis of experience. Descartes climbed into his foolish little stove and came out murmuring, *"Cogito, ergo sum."* While he might have made a more universally true statement had he said, "I suffer; therefore I am," nevertheless, his habit of doubting everything until given mathematical proof took hold and became *the* characteristic trait of the new science. Leibniz found life's meaning in the elucidation of innate ideas, and Locke had already laid a broad foundation for the revolt against religious authority. Whatever moral virtues we need could now be subject to the examination of reason, and to Locke this was the essence of religion. This opened a wide door to the comparative study of religions and introduced the discipline of the historical method and what Voltaire first called the "philosophy of history." This new discipline produced Hegel, and Spengler, and a new toleration. On the procession moved to help make a social consciousness in men like Shaftesbury, Coleridge, and Maurice; and in another echelon produced the deists, materialistic rationalism, French anthropocentrism, agnosticism, and the comparative newcomer logical positivism. The new induction was potent, even prolific, and has not run its race.

Man could endure the loss of his precious earth as the center of the universe; he could work by induction, even rejoicing in his escape from the authoritarianism of institutional systems of "truth." These he could stand so long as there remained to him the precious security of his own unique, aristocratic, natural supremacy over nature. But Charles Darwin read Laplace,[3] and then Lyell,[4] and knew the work of

[3] Pierre Simon de Laplace (d. 1827) on the development of solar systems from primitive nebulae.

[4] Sir Charles Lyell, the geologist (d. 1875).

his own grandfather,[5] and poured his prodigious capacity for detail into new molds. Leaving behind his beloved art and music, Darwin immersed himself in the bowels of the "Beagle," and there came out of his expeditions and his notes the death of the biological aristocrat. A *new method* appeared, and by its searching eye man appeared the same as all else organic, seemed subject to the laws that control the rest of nature. Riding hard on the heels of Darwin's "survival of the fittest" with all the misunderstanding of Huxley and Spencer added to confuse us, there burst another phenomenon.

A *new definition of man* came out of Nietzsche, Freud, and Marx. Strangely enough, a sick philosopher, a physician, and a hungry economist, none of whom ever knew either of the others, provided that combination of ideas that has effected the virtual collapse of the three powers within himself to which man could cling. In Nietzsche the conscience lost its power, in Freud the conscious was annihilated as the source of reasonable action, and in Marx personality lost its meaning.

All the while, from the early fifteen hundreds through the early days of the twentieth century, strange parallels in other realms accompanied the march of ideas. The *new nationalism* forced men to think of themselves as French or Dutch ahead of any other category. *New frontiers* opened more in one hundred years than the world had learned to master in a thousand years. The new politics found men claiming rights they had not known they had. The *new industrialism* was swallowing into its maw all kinds of human fodder and weaving in and over and through—the *new reformation*.

[5] Erasmus Darwin, naturalist (d. 1802).

93

Never reform, really, and not so completely religious as we have thought, the Reformation was a social, political, nationalistic, religious phenomenon like nothing the world had seen, though it brought nothing really new. Even its insistence on the right to examine its own heritage is a gift from outside itself.

And now in these latter days another new definition is upon us. Man will not leave even matter unexamined, and the *new matter* is the same as all matter; stuff is stuff, same stuff, and can be transformed to the basic concept—energy. The day of the physicist is well along and already on the near horizon; the day of the new god—the chemist—heralds its coming. The day comes—we will no longer eat the cadavers of dead animals and tubers that grow in the ground, heated and soaked with animal fat. We will instead inoculate ourselves, in a great central vein connected to our mighty brain and its one eye, with the amino acids the proteins used to make—back in the days when most men walked on two legs sometimes and did not rest half-prone on the electronically driven day beds that will move us from viewing screen to bed and back again, until our new rockets transfer us and our dominions to newer shores. Of such is the culture around us.

The Toughness of Culture

Since Hegel's *Philosophy of History* appeared in lecture form to his classes in the winter of 1822-23, and especially since Spengler's *Decline of the West* came out in 1918, a whole crowd of public speakers have been burying Western civilization. Petty politicians speak of the "end of civilization."

Crowd-haranguing itinerant preachers assure us that the "world is coming to an end." The kind of women's-club speakers that Sorokin calls "undertakers of culture" say the "Russians are coming." College presidents, ministers, newspaper columnists, along with the legendary Henny Penny, Ducky Lucky, and Goosey Loosey, join Chicken Little in her rush to tell the king that the sky is falling. It could be, but it never has, and the verdict of history so far has been that it was not the sky that fell on Chicken Little; it was acorns!

Indeed our agonies could be death agonies, but culture, civilizations, especially the kind built on the tough ideas that have framed our own, are infinitely tougher than these "clowns of the historical circus" assure us. Politicians, cliques, factions, armies, come and go. Some sort of culture persists.[6] A while ago I paid three dollars for a fourth-hand copy of the third English edition of the twelfth German edition of Rudolf Sohm's *Institutes of Roman Law.* One of my student friends spent his holiday at Christmas reading Homer's *Iliad.* Out at the seminary I have assigned Aristophanes' play *The Frogs* as a source of material for modern preaching. As Sorokin says, cultures do not die; only that unfit to live dies. Civilization is *tough,* and this is why it can lead into such strictures.

The Strictures of Culture

Culture can bind us. It can go awry, and once headed away, it has a tough mouth and will not respond to the bit. One's culture is most difficult to change. John Dewey says

[6] See Pitirim Sorokin, *The Crisis of Our Age* (New York: E. P. Dutton & Co., Inc., 1941), pp. 13-29.

that a man has as much chance of changing his culture as a baby's first words have of remaining in the family's vocabulary. Further, a man's culture is inescapable. Who can rise above his culture without denying it, and who can deny his own culture without being cut off, indeed?

Modern man is educated now. He can read. He reads philosophy, and even the man on the street now knows, says *The New Republic,*[7] that people are descended from monkeys; that the sun is made of radium; that Mars is inhabited by canal diggers; that the earth is getting hotter and will explode; that the earth is getting colder and will congeal; that the earth is getting drier and will blow away; that the earth will be smashed by running into a comet; that the average mental age of Americans is thirteen; that mankind, as a whole, is losing his teeth and his hair; that there is no soul; that there are two or three souls; that all rheumatism comes from bad teeth! Education will save us from these strictures of culture!

Even in his education, with everything the giants have given us, and they were giants, modern man is still caught in the strictures of his culture—caught like an aged Korean I saw holding the stump of his leg as he sprawled on a bridge in Seoul. A truck had just run him down; the leg was torn almost off. He sat there, clutching the spouting stump, looking awestruck at this thing that had happened to him, lost without the power of mobility, motion, movement. Alone, for none of the milling crowd in Seoul would

[7] E. E. Slosson, cited in *The New Republic,* XXXVII, 296.

touch him, he waited for the police, or some of his family, to accept the responsibility.

We are caught, too—caught in some strictures. In a world of personal frustrations, nameless longing, perverted destiny, we are not quite sure what to do with ourselves. Early on Sunday mornings, en route to what my deacons unfeelingly call "early Mass," I pass some inmates of a great mental hospital, out behind their high fence, pacing back and forth, unlit, half-exhausted cigarettes hanging limply, as they walk, and look and "think." Life is strange stuff; Socrates called it "terrible." We do not yet know how to keep it unsnarled. We are "stricted," restricted by time and space and our culture. We are bound, subject to the law of yesterday, subject to the "here and now," subject to the law of the neighbor, to life, and the great mysteries, disease, decline, and destiny. And as for death, we are not even sure what it is; we just know it is there, and the knowledge binds us.

In our strictures how smug and provincial we are. The great Bosanquet thought no earthquake would ever destroy London because God needed London more than Tokyo, for example.[8] A Siamese king put the new Dutch ambassador in the crazy ward when he happened to mention that in Holland men could walk across the canals in the wintertime. No ice in Siam! In Dayton, Ohio, when the word filtered back to the home town of the Wrights that Orville and Wilbur had done it, a man rose up to say, "That's not so; nobody ever flew, no one ever will, and if they should, it would not be anyone from Dayton!" How smug we are in our strictures. "What

---

[8] See Dixon, *op. cit.*, p. 80, for this and other examples.

bubbles we do blow," says Dixon in his Gifford Lectures. All of us are quite sure that the world is an enlarged copy of our own backyards. How blandly provincial we are, how smugly secure in our racisms and nationalisms.

Again, and still, how blandly all social groups assume their own superiority. How quickly we credit ourselves for merit and achievement. The Pueblo Indians of New Mexico called their mud walls the "center of the earth." We do it, too, and consequently have picked up a set of *cultural assumptions* so false and deadly as to create a cultural bind that threatens to make peace impossible.

Four hundred years ago Western white man began to be exposed to the vast reaches of a new frontier. Continents! Worlds! waited to be mastered and plundered. The old restrictions could not be imposed across that wide sea and that endless front. This meant *freedom,* or license, and our ancestors vaulted from their "foolish little caravels" to meet the challenges and openings of a new world. And now? Western man thinks he did it with his little hatchet—how grateful the world ought to be that we created this wealth and power with our little hatchet!

Western man has had tremendous energy, and great freedom, so far, but the tools he brought to the task? Where did he get his hatchet?

Columbus came to this hemisphere by means of an *Asiatic* sextant. The whole science of navigation is Asiatic in origin. The idea of latitude, the magnetic compass, astronomy, all are Asian. Along with arithmetic, algebra, quadratics, plane geometry, spherical geometry, trigonometry, our Arabic-

Hindu numerals, we are indebted for the construct zero, without which nothing mathematical is possible. In philosophy the Greeks learned from Asia, but it was all lost to the West except that Asiatics gave it back to us. Even the Greek New Testament came to us through the Asiatic hands of men like Averroës, Boethius, and others. In agriculture, from India to the Mediterranean, Asia knew deep contour plowing; Asiatics practiced irrigation and crop rotation when our German ancestors lived on meat and wild grain and our Scottish relatives were still eating each other on occasion. Anatomy came from Asia, for it was illegal to dissect in Europe for six hundred years after Asia knew the insides of the human body. Nine hundred years ago Asia had a modern pharmacopoeia, local anesthesia, quarantine, and surgery. Our vaunted ancestors learned even to bathe from Saracens during the crusades. Architecture, the cotton industry, asphalt paving, lamps, sugar, cosmetics, beds, divans, tables, chinaware, rugs, strawberries, peaches, ice cream, pepper, foods, metalcraft, horses, even our sportsmanship, all came out of Asia to us. Every day we use Arabic words: mattress, cotton, talcum, sugar, coffee, sherbet, naphtha, gypsum, benzine.[9]

The Christian faith is Asiatic! But a culture can so strict us we are capable of rejecting our own grandmother, *Asia*. How smug can a culture become?

There are lesser strictures that rise out of this cultural

[9] Toynbee, *A Study of History* (New York: Oxford University Press, 1946), Vol I. And see Henry Grady Weaver, *Mainspring* (Detroit: Talbot Books, 1947).

mélange, lesser only in that the point of seizure is the individual.

For example, in our smugness we are also involved in a mediocre sameness—a drab, everlastingly dull everydayness. We mouth the same truisms and platitudes, even at funerals. We use the same alibis, have the same reactions, advance the same ideas, urge ourselves toward the same shallow goals, and indulge ourselves in the same crazes, appetites, and whims—everywhere. The same fads attract us, we indulge the same weaknesses, and may God forgive us, we even tell the same jokes, and we do it over and over.

In our smug, strained sameness how can one fail to see our characteristic shallowness? Even our Gardens of Eden and our Utopias are so *easily* made perfect. I suspect that a cross section of the conscious desires of most congregations on most Sunday mornings would read: "Dear Lord, give us good roads for this afternoon's drive, and let our earthly journey be made joyful by a better expense account, new movies every day, and free drinks. And as we grow older, Lord, grant, we beseech thee, that longer vacations with pay, old-age retirement, unlimited credit, and easy payments may continue to bless us. In the ages to come grant us three Saturday nights a week, a color television set, along with hot and cold air conditioning in every room. This, for our soul's sake, we ask. Amen." Common man no longer moves by the invincible hopes of a race on the march—he is satisfied with his all-day sucker. The great mysteries—birth, death, the infinite secrets of our existence—no longer burden or attract. Heaven is realized every time one finds an unexpected parking place, the secrets of the universe simply add up to the latest electronic

100

gadget, and peace means luxury production. All but the slenderest of minorities of the billions who have walked across the boards of the stage, all but the very few have never known the show was playing; "we have been immersed in a struggle for temporal satisfactions and the pleasures of our senses," says Dixon. Most of us have died in the full tide of our sensualness, and all of us die in the full sweep of our ignorance, clutching the pebbles we gathered during our day on the beach, during which we never even saw the sea.

The resultant "human situation" is a "time out of joint." We become what we were never meant to be. No longer man—we are preoccupied, hurried, harassed. We are graspers, self-seekers, pushed by unworthy motives, based on unworthy hungers—no longer man. On the Santa Fe trail to Clovis I counted early one morning more than a hundred hawks, made for high free air, the chase, the kill of live warm meat, but they had grown fat and sluggish by living on the culture around them. Now they simply sat on fence posts waiting for some high-speeding Cadillac or Lincoln to chase, slaughter, and dress their morning rabbit for them. They were no longer hawks; they were vultures, and they moved and hopped and lived like vultures—not like hawks. In this "time out of joint" when we move and hop like something not man, "The Fear" is all around us. This is the heart of our stricture.

Afraid of silence, we create a din. To avoid the threat of loneliness, we live in a crowd. Afraid of unemployment, we hire ourselves to death. Threatened by work, we become slaves to machinery. Aware of the dangers of isolation, we join everything. Shocked by old age, we camouflage with make-up. Searching for rest, we drive ourselves to frenzy. Anxious for a break from the dullness of routine, we slaughter six hundred on a Labor Day week end. Seeking relaxation, we come up with nerves. We write "Peace of Mind" and turn suicide with an automatic. Uncertain of peace, we prepare for war. Until finally and inevitably, the only thing left to do is fight! The old adage holds, "Anything you prepare for you get!"

Fight? And what is left when a battle is over? I rode in a jeep with a major and a sergeant along trails not yet fully cleared of mines to see some crews on detached service. In a cluster of wild mountains north of Seoul we came to the nameless site of three nameless battles fought by nameless men. What is left when a fight is over? Even the memory of it gone with its last survivor, I could see just some splotches on a granite mountain where artillery had tried for range, some old holes, stacks of unexpended and dangerous ammunition, duds from bazookas, seventy-fives, and mines, dangerous antipersonnel mines, along with twenty-five unidentifiable skeletons of some North Koreans in that little pocket there. No man knew the name of the place he died. He died to keep some other fellows from using a dirt road.

And what is left when the battle is over? At the big base hospital our Air Force operates at Tachikawa we took in more than a thousand, battered and split, after the siege of Dien Bien Phu. Shortly after their evacuation to France I walked through the wards with the Negro nurse who had been supervisor during their occupancy. "Captain," I said, "your wards are spotless; there is nothing soiled, no odors, no trace of the agonies of a thousand Legionnaires. Do these 'fighting devils' leave nothing behind them?" "Oh, yes," she answered, soft-voiced, as if to herself, "they leave behind an unbelievable capacity for affection and a record of incredible courage, but that is all."

That is all—unbelievable affection and incredible courage, and in this crazy, confused stricture of culture everyone is homesick—homesick for something he does not know—and this is the most poignant of our strictures.

All over the Eastern theater this is the universal sickness—homesickness. From colonel to airman it is "samo-samo." On gun emplacements, in crash boats on the Yellow Sea, in plane cockpits, or on garbage trucks and bulldozers, at the guardhouse and in colonels' quarters, he tells you about it. All night long, a fine-looking Canadian, mustache and kilts, executive officer of the famous Black Watch Regiment, the Royal Canadian Highlanders, sits opposite you in a rattling Japanese coach and tells of the three years his memories of home have kept him living like a father and husband should. High over the Pacific in the dark, a lonely young Marine tells how homesick he is for his six sisters and the orphans' home in Texas where they all grew up. And you ask, "What is this cloud of homesickness that covers the earth and wraps up a man in any crowded city street?" Is it that we are all too subjective, too brooding, too babyish? Or is it that we are really longing for some *highest value* around which our lives can center, but our culture cuts us off? And as you brood over that stricture of culture, a line from somewhere in the myriad lines of Thomas Wolfe begins to haunt you: An old man, dying in a cold train compartment, rumbling along in the Austrian night, talks as he dies, "Now I go no more. Eferyvere it iss ze same. . . . Fields, hills, mountains, riffers, cities, peoples—you vish to know about zem all. Vun field, vun hill, vun riffer, . . . zat iss enough! . . . Vun life, vun place, vun time." [10]

And so, we look for home. "Where is my home?" cries Nietzsche, almost wildly. Where can my highest values center? Where is that place I long for by nature and my culture denies to me? We look for home, and ironically we run against a deadly substitute for home our culture has built.

SUPERFICIAL CHRISTIANITY

The force that does most to keep us from home here in the West is superficial Christianity. In form it is an idolatry and may appear as a tribalism, a naturalism, or even a culturalism, such as the Neo-Fascism in the United States which has found a home in some so-called Christian circles. This idolatrous form has its theology, its ethic, and its philosophy of history. It wears the habiliments of the faith, uses the symbols, vocabulary, dogma, and discipline of the real thing. It mistakes discipline for discipleship; it substitutes language of the Book for the meaning of the Word. Because of its false idea of value superficial Christianity is preoccupied with means, techniques, tools, rather than end, goal, or God. The tool becomes an end, a slogan becomes law, a pattern becomes the original, and the *status quo* is sacred. Superficial Christianity, built on false values, is geometric rather than alge-

---

[10] "Dark in the Forest" in *From Death to Morning* (New York: Chas. Scribner's Sons, 1935), p. 109. Used by permission of the publisher.

braic; that is, it draws up pretty patterns and ignores vital relationships. Outward form is more important than inner renewal. It builds what Merrill Hutchins has called a "holy-roller Catholicism" out of the freedom of the gospel. It equates denomination and Kingdom. Participation is equivalent to consecration, enrollment equals redemption, enthusiasm is the unfailing flag of the Holy Spirit, opinion is conviction, "program" is gospel, any "idea" is by revelation, means is end, scheme of work is divine decree, and the voice of the people is the voice of God which is why superficial Christianity is so deathly afraid of criticism. Hence, superficial Christianity takes on the color of its environment, preaches its "unexamined concepts." It does not care for books and work. It excuses any kind of shoddy workmanship that can be covered over with pious intention. It confuses commotion with motion, sells tickets for merry-go-rounds, gets fat on lip service and cliché-filled pronouncements, all the while pre-empting the place of a valid center of value by denying the tragedy, suffering, and tension-ridden agonies of this present world.

This superficial Christianity not only obscures our center of reference; it actually seeks to escape the possibility of being confronted by a valid center. Hence, superficial Christianity is everywhere an attempt to escape both Christ and the present moment in history. But superficial Christianity is clever. It will not admit to its attempt to escape Christ. It strives instead *to escape the present,* prattling about Christ all the while. It goes off from this present moment, witlessly waving its charts, maps, and sacred chronologies of the future, but this is a subterfuge. The real purpose is to escape the heavy

105

demands of Christ in the present by seeking evening time before the morning's work is done. Or it goes off just as witlessly into the past, seeking its validation in "trails of blood," living on historical bias that strains even the "daisy chains of bishops," refusing to demonstrate its living center in the here and now. Or, and most tragically, it *joins its culture* in escaping Christ by simple retreat from the frontiers of the present. It seeks relief from the tensions by forsaking the crossroads of this world's agonies. It finds the defense of the crossroads downtown to be too costly and has resolved to hold only the suburban side streets. It denies its crossway by taking refuge in the necessity of the material, and lots of it. It never really confronts the terrors of any moment; it pulls always toward the slower currents and less violent needs of the economically, racially, ideologically "safe" ones. This withdrawing action it camouflages so that it never has to be confronted by its own errors. Content with the statistical summaries of its bishops and boards, superficial Christianity never really grapples with anything, no main issues, and certainly not its own errors and failures. It simply refuses to see the ghosts that are there except when it has canonized them by declaring some special day to think about them and receive an offering.

So, like blind guides, taking rest in walled cities, self-emasculated to avoid the fires of passion, self-deafened to avoid the noise of the conflict the Cross wages outside the walls of our refuges, superficial Christianity takes its timid journey, and as it goes, it adapts, minimizes, externalizes, chauvinizes, and idolizes; it avoids by substitution, diversion, or denial the scandal of the Cross, the sacrifice of self, with-

106

out which there is no real Christianity. Speaking always within its culture, it may even be vehemently condemnatory and vociferously pious in its preachments and at the same time be a waste and desolation. Its patterns deny Christian ethics, and its doctrinaire deity has no connection with the living God of true theology and experience. And sadly, only at the crossroad agonies of death, loss, sin, or great grief do the adherents of superficial Christianity begin to wonder what it is they have missed all the time. "O Zarathustra . . . it eateth me up. . . . '*Where* is—*my* home?' " [11]

Under such strictures does the culture that surrounds bind us: the strictures of life itself, of the finite world, are no more formidable than the sameness, shallowness, and smugness, the provincialisms, prejudices, and false religions that lead us to such unworthy centers. The falcon that is our culture bides his time, and he can afford to soar there, waiting. His victim is bound, and in this human situation we all share the strictures. We are homesick for the valid center of life's meaning that would free us.

THE FREEDOM OF RELEASE

There was a leader once who drove a coach and horses, roughshod, through all the hoary regulations of his culture. He left deep tracks across the smooth surfaces of traditionalism and formalism. He laughed at our legalisms and our lesser sacraments, and his rude steps shattered the sacred pavement of our most precious institutionalisms and our prejudiced bigotries. He was a blazing revolutionist, a stout-hearted

[11] Friedrich Nietzsche, *Thus Spake Zarathustra*, IV, lxix, *The Shadow*.

fighter, and we could take that. But his tools were different: love and a kingdom of love, so we tried to kill him. He overthrew our tables, scattered our coins and livestock, cast out our devils, forgave our prostitutes, and withal, displayed such an unholy disregard for our pigs, law, and culture that we were sure he came from Satan. Then he called our best churchmen a "generation of vipers," and our hatred hung out on the line for all to see. He slapped our dead religion and claimed we could not really tell what a fellow is by the way he looks; and worse, he consorted with publicans, sinners, and Samaritans. He insisted that our cultural standards were invalid where they denied human personality its potential, and he rejected the stuff and nonsense of religion so vehemently that it shattered the Temple calm. Worst of all, he claimed the primacy of personality so completely that he rejected even the eternity of our Temple walls, claimed that God does not have to have us, said he would give us a better Temple, and wound up with his glove almost in the face of our high priest! And to all this we had varying reactions.

One of our best men had a reaction strange to us. He was standing by that day in the Temple, and he heard and saw it all. In his distinguished career he had heard and seen many things, but we are sure he had never heard anyone question the eternity of our Temple walls before. It seemed to us that what he heard the Galilean say did something to our man Nicodemus. As he turned away from that scene in the Temple court, it seemed to us that his eyes were saying, "What confidence, what at-homeness, with what assurance does this commoner call our Temple his Father's house!" To tell the truth, Nicodemus looked to us like a man whose heart sud-

denly knows a haunting longing. He acted like a man who realized he had lost forever something he had but barely glimpsed and still desperately wanted. He turned away from there like a man suddenly pressed down by the weight of his whole culture.

We heard later that Nicodemus actually went to see the commoner that night, and we still cannot understand it. What could Nicodemus want? He has everything! He is not a man of sin; he is not of low character, nor of immoral habit, nor even of poor education. In our minds he has everything, and we judge him to be the best kind of man our religion can make—cultured, loyal, high-minded, generous, and devoutly religious. He has the social power of respect, influence, and position. He is "Master of Israel," and the prestige of the Supreme Court is with him. In addition this man is clean, superior, reserved, dignified, rich. He has all his culture can give him—all the best his time can bestow—but he seemed like one who is hungry. And this morning one of us said he was certain about it—that he passed Nicodemus and the commoner at dusk, sitting on a low wall; and further, that he heard Nicodemus lean across to say words strange to us:

"We know you come from God—a teacher." Now why would he do that? Why would Nicodemus go to see any teacher? He *is* a teacher. Certainly we can understand a man's momentary search for something beyond his own institution, but why would Nicodemus go to a strange teacher? He is one of us, and besides what can a fellow do? It's a puzzle to us that a man like Nicodemus would go to Jesus.

And now across the centuries, caught, stricted within our

own culture, caught like Nicodemus, we still do not understand what brought him there. We join the querulous friend of Nicodemus to ask for ourselves:

What else can a man do except be born in his flesh, be taken to church and baptized? What else can a man do except follow the pattern his elders have set until at last he knows how to do religious things in his own name? What else can a man do except learn when to genuflect, how to hold his hands before the wafer is given and after, how to keep his mind on the stations of the prayer, until at last he recognizes for himself the mystery, miracle, and authority of the ceremonial? What else can a man do when he has been moral and confessed it, when he has paid his tithe and gone a-pilgriming? What else can he do when he has been to worship, supported the seasonal notions of his church, and has made a friend of his pastor?

What else? Nothing, we have found, except to stifle his inquiring mind and smother the writhings of his free spirit by rejoicing in a "mystery" he cannot understand. Nothing, we have found, except to give over his own responsibilities to a professional clergyman and an institution made sacred by the hope of our hearts.

There is no place to go, Nicodemus. One cannot escape his culture. Become what the pattern demands and you will be "Christian" and safely within the walls of your culture. That is always the answer of the Nicodemus religion, but it leaves its cold and vicious hungers.

Yet this new pilgrim Nicodemus will not stop. His short questions burst with hidden meanings. How can a man enter

another time into that comfortable prenatal darkness? How can a man get rid of his experience and his scars? How can a man become what he desperately needs to become? Where can he be new again? How can he be what he never needed to be before? Where can he go to rise above his culture that binds him? Is there a place on earth or in heaven or in hell where a man can escape time? Where is there relief from this cosmic burden that presses and this monotonous, hypnotizing, fascinating "tick, tick, tick," of the droplets of life? Is there a place or a state or a way that a man may be rid of time and decay and what the strictures of his precious culture do to his soul?

The commoner's marvelous answer makes short work of all our fantastic desires to escape time and our culture. He says simply: "Flesh is flesh." That is to say, flesh is *just* flesh, always was *just* flesh, never will be more than *just* flesh. Carrion is carrion; flesh is always dying flesh and therefore must make terms with time and culture. "Spirit is spirit," he adds. Which is to say, the spirit alone goes beyond. It is of the spirit that a man escapes time and rises above the strictures of his culture. It is a *birth,* Nicodemus, for birth is always spiritual process. It means something more than your lifelong participation in things of flesh; it means more than a certain way of acting within a certain institution; it means more than belonging to a certain race, practicing a particular code, or living within a certain culture. It is of the spirit that a man escapes himself, time, and the strictures of his culture. And because it it a spirit process, it is a birth, Nicodemus. There is no better way to symbolize it.

111

(Tall and handsome in her sixty years, turned gray in the service of mankind, immaculately groomed gentlewoman, she stood at the door of our hospital room and said, "In spite of delivering over ten thousand babies and teaching medical students these twenty years, I am still filled with awe and wonder at the spiritual nature of natural birth.")

Cleansing and Committal

A birth is always a *cleansing*—the cleansing from the old receptacle that has held the new. It is the tearing away of that that has enclosed. It is the agonized separation of the living from the dying. It is the torturous release of that flesh that cannot hold back the new life force. Anyone who has ever helped a tiny calf or colt into the world knows that birth is a cleansing of the new from the old. The separation of life from older flesh is always cleansing.

And because of its nature birth is also *committal.* There is no birth, no continuing new life, until there is the committal of the born one to the new arena of life. No tiny baby is alive on its own, none is really born, until the valves in its heart close over to permit the fluttering muscle to begin its long task of pumping its own blood through its own veins.

This, even in the flesh, is a spiritual thing if it is a birth. Only by such a cleansing from the old mothering receptacle and by committal to the new arena can flesh make terms with time. This is the reason men must be "born from above"; this is why men must become as little children. It is the only way we can come to terms with time. Men become as children to whom time is no problem, for to a child everything is just beginning. By this birth, Nicodemus, a man be-

112

comes newborn, a child, and then: failure is beginning; loss is beginning; defeat, old age, frustration, the scars of one's culture, are all beginnings, not dead ends. The final curtain becomes an opening overture; the complimentary close is a salutation; finale and epilogue are the introduction to the beginning. All of time stretches before the unbounded boyhood of the newborn one to whom flesh and its strictures become means to an end.

Committal and Cross

Birth is never enough. This is the agony of Christendom, that the birth has been kept subjective and uninvolved in the cleavages of the culture around us. By the terms of the new committal a man cannot submit to being lifted out of his flesh-time stricture as an individual. Rather, he dashes back inside the wreckage in a grand acceptance of responsibility for the culture he did not create. He joins the race, the human race, and this is the meaning of Cross in the Nicodemus story. The birth requires a *demonstration,* even for the Master of birth. Indeed, here, he shows us how.

Nicodemus still cannot understand it. Once more comes his urgent cry: "How can it be? You say flesh is flesh and always will be flesh. I know that now. But *how* can a man get out of his agony of time and flesh and become what he is not? How can a man be born when he is old?"

And the commoner answers: "A man is born again when cleansed like water cleanses, committed like the spirit commits, he comes to accept the banner God raises up for him to follow—for as Moses lifted up the serpent. . . ."

113

After the great cry of Nicodemus I feel a great stillness falling between them. Still bewildered, only half-born, Nicodemus sits and reviews the pressures that have brought him to this new teacher. Then, at length, he speaks, slowly, his mind back in the Temple with the Jews and the scene of the day before: "Teacher, that was a tremendous thing you did in the Temple yesterday. It is a thing no one ever did before. It was as if a man had literally thrown away the confines of his own culture! Is that what you meant when you spoke of destroying our Temple?"

And the commoner answers: "Nicodemus, I meant my act and my word to say that this prostitution and perversion of truth would see any culture destroyed. It is already dead! And I have something nobler to put in its place!"

"But, Rabbi! if you act like that once more in the Temple, there will not be any way you can give us a better release. This kind of thing can only issue in your death, and then where is your new birth of the spirit? Do you see, Rabbi, if you continue to oppose Jewry, your own culture, that the men of whom I am one will take you apart, piece by piece, thinking they do God a service?

And Jesus answers: "Dear Nicodemus, can it not penetrate to your mind that my death is the *means,* the one way the new birth and the new temple can come to men?" Then he whispers to Nicodemus there in the gathered friendly darkness: "Isaiah seemed to know this. Go back to your synagogue and see how he promised a banner would be lifted. Whatever Isaiah meant, I am that banner that says a *man has got to be committed, involved, even emptied, made dead!* There is no new birth without this commitment, this acceptance of

114

responsibility for the culture I did not cause and the sin I did not do. For me and for mine it is the only way. And I, if I be lifted up from the earth, will draw all men unto me."

Did Nicodemus get it? Who knows? At least we cannot forget that in that later nighttime, when men stood around that cross regretting it, it was this half-converted pilgrim of the night, the one who shared this long converse with the commoner, who went to Pontius Pilate to get the body of that dead rabbi—and like the one dead, Nicodemus was accepting the agonies, sins, and strictures of his whole culture when he did it! So must we all. New birth is not birth without the commitment.

Cross and Cultural Redemption

Once this comes alive, it does something to that Christianity now so involved in the strictures of its culture. Its spokesmen come alive. We are no longer guilty of that "dreary drip of desultory declamation." We begin to preach, as Bunyan, "what I did feel, what I smartingly did feel." We waste no time on generalities, but bearing our own involvement of cross and culture, we make straight for the pew. We no longer mouth a vague diffusion of amiability. We will begin to speak as men under the hammer that breaks the rock of our pride in pieces. We will confess, as we speak, our own failure to accept the responsibility for the culture we inherit and pass on. We will recognize the paucity and insufficiency of our individual redemption and begin to address ourselves to that deadly corporeity of cultural evil we have so long ignored. And if we are ourselves involved in the Cross

115

we preach, who knows but that even our own culture will learn that culture is under judgment, for culture will listen if a gospel is *relevant*.

We will ask men to join the human race by recognizing the inevitable forces at work to humble us all. We will forget our shallow gospel that is one long drawn out Tut! Tut! and begin to share the burden of being dying men with every person we pass. We will call out to passers-by, with Kierkegaard, "Why are all of you so content to live in the cellar when there are rooms upstairs?" And some of them will catch it and begin to clamber out.

They can learn that the Christian gospel does not need to go on tiptoeing past that deadly corporate evil, that evil that is more than the sum total of our individual sin. They will be braced to accept the burden of the knowledge that there is need for more than individual redemption. They will speak of the redemption of culture, of civilization, of *churches,* and of *nations.* And they will do this because they recognize that the deadly corporeity of our evil brings judgment not only on us but on our corporations, institutions, shrines, idols, and sacred values.

And one fine day
men will begin to repent for sins
they did not do
because they have already accepted responsibility
for the culture they did not create.

And this is the key to the release within one's culture: A man begins to repent for the sins he did not do; he becomes responsible for a vast and evil sea not of his own making; and like his Master, he lets it put him on a cross. He recognizes

that committees and councils and churches and governments cannot and do not repent. He repents *for* them. He knows he cannot repent for Genghis Khan, Hannibal, or Alexander; he cannot repent for Napoleon and Bismarck, but he can repent for Hitler and Mussolini and Stalin, as well as Churchill, Roosevelt, and Truman, even Eisenhower. And he can do it because he is under judgment because of his own unfaced responsibility for the unfaced evil that exists in his own time. He becomes responsible for the provincial ego that brands his own denomination; he becomes responsible for the limited vision of that nation which will not take its place among the children of earth and of God but intends to lord it over all creation. He becomes responsible for remaining where he is. He becomes responsible for the sin of his own limited provincialisms that he caught from his forebears and wishes to keep. He becomes responsible for the sin of his own family, environment, and the generation to which he is debtor.

This is the only way that the Christian faith can speak to the deadly civilizational evil that surrounds us. It is a matter for each and for me. I begin to clamber out of the pit I did not dig and in which I will not stay. A man's whole life becomes a process of accepting responsibility for sin he did not do and climbing on a ladder of repentance out of a pit he did not dig in order that he might pay a debt he never promised.

CHAPTER FOUR

FAITH and the VULTURE

 *I knew it would come before we parted, Victor, and it did. Even when we met later in Kentucky, it was never quite the same as that last day when we talked of Death, the vulture who gets everything.*
After this day we had talked of the Ultimate, so what is there left to say?

The red snow of Lidice was fresh in your mind; I could still weep at the thought of my best boyhood friend dead in his chute straps over the hedgerows in Belgium. Perhaps we were closest together here, for your confessed nihilism had a hunger born of desire to believe, and my half-born gospel had a seam where doubt sprouted and leaned toward you, so we shared at least a common doom. But that was years ago, and I had not then been so pressed by Death.

And when we meet in Switzerland (soon now, I promise), it will not be the same at all. Bright sun, crisp and cold, a fire on your hearth, blue lake through the windows, smiles and big laughter and serious talk, but it will not be the same. We will have finished our talk of Death, and what is there left to say?

FAITH AND THE VULTURE

*My life is a mystery, but death
is a dark malady which faith cannot evade.
Yet faith has a word;
it speaks of process and purpose
of which death is a part,
and it speaks of something steady
over all the wreckage.*

WHAT DOES IT MATTER who wrote it? The agony of everyman is in it.

Oak Ridge
September

. . . . if you find these lines bleak, know that we sometimes think of death, even in laboratories. . . . His death is a desolation and waste I cannot soften. Mind-clenching work went into his doctorate which he accomplished without any help beyond the old Doctor's letter. I do not know what to make of the circumstances

121

—he was too well trained to get caught. . . . On the other hand he was that one in hundreds who could have. . . . He was a steel wire, full of a fierce, stubborn will. As boys we fought, and I never really won, and he never said the word I tried to make him say, and I think now he never said it to anybody.

Now he is dead. He never reached inside a human body to lift a life out of shadow; he never fulfilled the promise that was in him. . . . I cannot feel that he will ever take up that broken piece of work, not he, that one particular boy I knew.

Can the fact that we live mean no more than that he was once alive? I cannot let him be an incident. . . .

Yours,

Beginning where you are, life is strange stuff—unique. The thought of leaving it behind is abhorrent to us; we want it, we cling to it. Even the tears of the human race with which the earth is soaked from crust to center do not take away our zest for life nor prepare us for that shocking first encounter with death. In *Back to Methuselah*, George Bernard Shaw brings Adam and Eve upon a fawn, neck broken and dead:

Adam. Dead? What word is that?
Eve. Like that. I call it dead.
Adam. There is something uncanny about it.
Eve. Oh! it is changing into little white worms.
Adam. Throw it into the river. It is unbearable.
Eve. I dare not touch it.
Adam. Then I must, though I loathe it. It is poisoning the air.[1]

What does it mean to be alive? What does it mean to be

[1] Used by permission of The Public Trustee and The Society of Authors.

dead? If we could know what life is, perhaps we would have a better clue to the meaning of death. As it is, we love life supremely, and even the devil in Faust admits that "blood is a juice of very special kind."

Life can go sour, become fermented and sick, and still be good. Even when life smells like Thomas Wolfe's Brooklyn, it is good.[2] Children are children in narrow-streeted tenements too, and do not like to go to bed. Everything that lives strives for life. The *élan vital* will not let us gladly die, except in the agonies of fatigue and grief and insanity. Not for many has the thought of death been attractive. So Mephistopheles muses,

> And yet, methinks, by most 'twill be confessed
> That Death is never quite a welcome guest.[3]

He is, rather, a constant threat.

THE THREAT OF DEATH

Nature knows the threat of death, and this is why she is so prodigal with her seed. The threat of death is the meaning of nature's wastefulness. She does not mean to make an oak for every acorn but to feed wild deer as well. But what of this awful waste in terms of personality? Did nature intend to make 9,999 human beings every time she made one man? Does she really need to be so prodigal with her seed?

The threat of death is the meaning of waste, and the threat is everywhere there are human beings. This is the meaning

[2] "No Door" *op. cit.*
[3] Goethe, *Faust.*

123

of our wastefulness—the waste that covers all the beaches of the world's vast seas—the waste that clutters the beaches of all our human hearts and ways. The threat is everywhere and becomes actuality in every form of waste.

That way of life which bids you be content if you are competently fed, watered, housed, and amused is a waste and a death. It deracinates us by hordes and casts up as refuse on the beaches the millions who put down no common roots nor continuing ties with anything of value. They are waste; they are dead.

That dread disease, that cancer of colossality, which makes us rely on sheer quantity, bigness, size, takes its rise from this threat of death. But that is waste and death, for in present-day civilization men and cities may flourish and be big with promise that do not rest on a single continuing value or virtue. This is death and the threat of death, not progress.

That waste and sham that diverts institutions and their constituencies of believers to continuing concern over inconsequentials, that "inertia of institutionalized mediocrity which holds fast bound the hosts of God," it is shameful waste and a form of the death that surrounds us. The mother love, twisted by personal desires, the wasted husbandhood and fatherhood, the manpower that never did grow up, the women who have never and now never can achieve that for which they were made; along with the sheer utter insanity of that purposelessness in life which produces such waste-death everywhere there are people; they are flotsam, jetsam, washed up by unnoticed little hurricanes on every bay and beach.

At the bottom of it all is death. To faith death is *the* enemy. "Death is at the bottom of every evil passion. Pride,

greed, ambition are deadly in their results. There is no other evil in the world except death. . . ."[4] Death is the ultimate threat; all of us live in the teeth of the three *D*'s; disease, decay, death. So what is there left to say?

Tolstoy, facing it, breaks down with, "I stand like a fool on this dizzy height, understanding clearly that there is nothing in life, that there never was anything, and never will be."[5] It is a universal threat, "the same leaky bottom in these wild waters bears us all,"[6] and what is there left to say? The threat is universal and inevitable.

In that immortal reportorial *French Revolution,* Thomas Carlyle reaches heights he never afterward reaches when he speaks of the parade of death:

Sovereigns die and Sovereignties; how all dies. . . . The Merovingian Kings, have all wended slowly on,—into Eternity. Charlemagne sleeps at Salzburg, only Fable expecting that he will awaken. Charles the Hammer, Pepin Bow-legged, where now is their eye of menace, their voice of command? Rollo and his shaggy northmen . . . have sailed on a longer voyage. The hair of Towhead needs no combing; Iron-Cutter cannot cut a cobweb; shrill Fredegonda, shrill Brunhilda, have had out their hot life-scold, . . . they are all gone; sunk,—down, down, with the tumult they made; and the rolling and trampling of ever new generations pass over them; and they hear it not anymore forever.[7]

"Wa! Wa! . . . the wild Clotaire groaned out, . . . 'what

[4] Berdyaev, *The Destiny of Man,* p. 320. Used by permission of Geoffrey Bles Ltd.

[5] Tolstoy, *My Confession.*

[6] Carlyle.

[7] Pp. 7-8.

great God is this that pulls down the strength of the strongest kings?'" In the Parisian parade Carlyle comes across Abbe Maury: "Thou shalt have a Cardinal's hat, and plush and glory; but alas, also, in the long run—mere oblivion, like the rest of us; and six feet of earth!" [8]

Even though it happens on a stage, the death of young Hotspur in Henry IV is no less real. Harry speaks to the corpse of his rival:

> Ill-weaved ambition, how much art thou shrunk!
> When that this body did contain a spirit,
> A kingdom for it was too small a bound;
> But now two paces of the vilest earth
> Is room enough.[9]

So what is there left to say? Even though modern man has almost forgotten it, nature means to kill him, as Durant said, and will likely be successful. Are we not as represented in Tolstoy's tale? [10]

A traveler in the wild country is attacked by a furious wild beast. To save himself the traveler gets into a waterless well, but at the bottom of it he sees a dragon with its jaws wide open to devour him. The unhappy man dares not get out for fear of the wild beast and dares not descend for fear of the dragon, so he catches hold of the branch of a wild plant growing in a crevice of the wall. His arms grow tired, and he feels that he must soon perish, death awaiting him on either side, but he still holds on; and he sees two mice, one black

---

[8] *Ibid.,* pp. 20, 117.

[9] Shakespeare, *King Henry IV*, Part I, Act V, scene 4.

[10] See Tolstoy's version of this Asiatic fable, *op. cit.*

and one white, gradually making their way round the stem of the wild plant on which he is hanging, nibbling it through. The plant will soon give way and break off, and he will fall into the jaws of the dragon. The traveler sees this and knows that he must inevitably perish; but while still hanging, he looks around him and finding some drops of honey on the leaves of the wild plant, he stretches out his tongue and licks them.

So what is there to say? With keener pain than any I know, Thomas Wolfe saw it:

There has been life enough, and power, grandeur, joy enough, and there has also been beauty enough, and God knows there has been squalor and filth and misery and madness and despair enough; murder and cruelty and hate enough, and loneliness enough to fill your bowels with substance of gray horror, and to crust your lips with its hard and acrid taste of desolation.

And oh, there has been time enough, even in Brooklyn there is time enough, strange time, dark secret time enough, dark million-visaged time enough, forever flowing by you like a river, even in cellar-depths in Brooklyn there is time enough, but when you try to tell the man about it you cannot, for what is there to say? [11]

Sometimes, among less sensitive men consciousness begins to awaken to this threat that surrounds us. A man finds himself stirred by it; he realizes he has been busy with many things; now they pall on him; he is no longer quite sure they were worth the doing; he knows they occupy him, but he cannot say why they do; he runs frantically for amusement and diversion, yet no kind of elaborate routine amuses. To do

[11] "No Door," *op. cit.,* p. 12. Used by permission of Chas. Scribner's Sons.

one thing after another seems now no better than to do any other thing; in short he finds nothing to do that is better than to do nothing at all. Until comes the crisis: life is fragile, death is certain, and like Richard a man senses its eve and there are moments when

> The lights burn blue. It is now dead midnight.
> Cold fearful drops stand on my trembling flesh.

And what is there left to say?

Now the red light fades swiftly from the old red brick of rusty houses, and there are voices in the air, and somewhere music, and we are lying there, blind atoms in our cellar-depths, gray voiceless atoms in the manswarm desolation of the earth, and our fame is lost, our names forgotten, our powers are wasting from us like mined earth, while we lie here at evening and the river flows . . . and dark time is feeding like a vulture on our entrails, and we know that we are lost, and cannot stir . . . and there are ships there! there are ships! . . . and Christ! we are all dying in the darkness! [12]

So what is there left to say? Each man faces his private dead-end street; it is for him the end of the age.

PATTERNS OF ENCOUNTER

Some men meet death grandly, a speech in hand; some talk as if going to a long-delayed banquet; some sputter in the face of death like a wet fuse; here and there one is impatient and belligerent. Others are bewildered; some are stoic or attempt to be philosophical about it. There are dignity and grace in the death of some, and there is fear or a torrent

[12] *Ibid.,* p. 14.

of terror for others. There are patterns in the way men die.

"Thou hast invited me to Thy table, Lord; and behold I come. . . ." said John the evangelist.[13] "Lord, now is the time to arise and go! The good time which I welcome, which is Thy will; the hour when I must leave my exile, and my soul shall enjoy the fulfillment of all her desire!" cried Teresa, the saint of Avila. In contrast, a man like Mussolini needed more time. "But . . . but . . . Mr. Colonel," he sputtered as they dragged him to his wall. Le Comte says that when an old minister told the famed Revolutionary hero and devout leader Ethan Allen that the angels were waiting for him, the old man exploded. "Waiting, are they? Waiting, are they? Well, . . . let 'em wait." "Too bad! It's too late!" murmured Beethoven when the wine he had requested finally came. "I do not understand what I have to do," muttered Tolstoy as he died. Marie Antoinette apologized to her executioner; she had stepped on his foot. Charles II spoke of his mistress, Nell Gwyn. "Welcome, Sister Death," cried Francis of Assisi. But few have left behind them last words as filled with dignity and grace as those of an Indian chief named Crowfoot, leader of the Blackfoot Confederacy:

A little while and I will be gone from among you, whither I cannot tell. From nowhere we come, into nowhere we go. What is life? It is a flash of a firefly in the night. It is a breath of a buffalo in the winter time. It is as the little shadow that runs across the grass and loses itself in the sunset.[14]

[13] According to Edward S. Le Comte, *Dictionary of Last Words* (New York: Philosophical Library, 1955), p. 120 and reviewed in *Time*, January 17, 1955.

[14] *Ibid.*, p. 58.

There are those whose approach to death is the pattern of ignorance. They see neither the dragon nor the mice in Tolstoy's fable. They only lick the honey for a while; something directs their gaze to the dragon and the mice, and they quit tasting the honey. "From these I could learn nothing," says Tolstoy; "we cannot unknow what we do know." [15]

There is the Epicurean pattern: seek the honey in spite of dragon and mice. "Then I commended mirth," says the writer of Ecclesiastes, but not many men have a thousand wives to divert them from death, and for every man with a harem there are a thousand without any wife at all to join in on the merrymaking.

Here and there, and at an astonishing level in the Western world, there are those who adopt the pattern of strength and energy toward death. When life seems to be evil and absurd, destroy it! But mostly we do not go in for genocide, except by war and automobile, or for suicide, except by indirection. By and large, men adopt the pattern of weakness: We endure life, knowing most of it has bad spots, and we wait for death, knowing it is no good.

This produces the master pattern for facing and enduring the presence of death in our time. The master plan is camouflage: throw a sheet over the whole business. Put a wreath and "Do not disturb" on the entryway. And how does this pattern face death?

We build Forest Lawns and Rest Havens with angels and harps and stone benches for spirits to sit on. We rely on the calm, professional, half-smiling air of undertakers to ease us through. We want striped pants, carnations in the attendants'

[15] *Op. cit.*

130

button holes, Cadillac coaches and rubber shock absorbers on the casket rollers, with imitation grass and flowers to cover up the sight of the good clean earth.

Or we build so-called mausoleums, another kind of tree, to keep everything aboveboard. We count on marcels, finger waves, and cosmetology; pajamas for the "Reclining Room" and gray or lavender gowns for coffin-wear. We feature old-rose draperies and the hushed and peaceful look. But the camouflage appears best at the funeral itself when the mourners pass the bier. There we are at our very best: the averted eye that will not look at death; or its alternate, the tiptoe bypass that comes this way because it is the only door; the bold familiar look of the one who attends many funerals and enjoys them; or the absent one who "wanted to remember"; the one who always says, "John was his own worst enemy," or, "Poor Joe; he never thought he'd go," or, "How nice he looks," or always, "It didn't look like Pete." And the last one, the one who always tells you that this man who loved life, wanted to be well, to live, is "better off"!

So what is there left to say? We go on excusing ourselves for death as if all death were suicide and we could stop it if we would. No! We are caught on a treadmill—and unless some Hand from outside us comes to our rescue, what is there left to say?

CHALLENGE TO DEATH

"Death, be not proud. . . . Death, thou shalt die," [16] and this is the challenge of faith, but it requires some explication.

[16] John Donne, *Holy Sonnets,* X.

131

Somewhere in a sermon of John Donne's he recalls the ancient maps of old explorers and caught an illustration:

It is said of old *Cosmographers,* that when they had said all that they knew of a Countrey, and yet much more was to be said, they said that the rest of those countries were possest with *Giants,* or *Witches,* or *Spirits,* or *Wilde beasts,* so that they could pierce no farther into that Countrey.[17]

We have peopled and powered the land beyond our limit of exploration with all kinds of wondrous creatures, fearsome and horrendous, or fair and angelic. Yet this fact remains: Only those who have traveled a country are qualified to describe it. "Of death only the dead can speak with any authority." [18] That is to say, the meaning of death can be given only by the dead. Faith escapes the effrontery of discussing unknowable death by its claim that its source of information is the "dead." All of faith's claims and challenges are based squarely on "that One who died and is alive," nor has faith found any reason to change her memory of what he said *before* he had crossed the river. But faith will not be too specific in her venture, and faith will claim the right to learn as she advances from any who will teach her. She makes her observations and deductions as she goes, and so intimidated is she by the vastness of her unknowables that she cannot be badgered into marking off a "Countrey" she has not reached. "He that asks me what heaven is, meanes not to heare me, but to silence me; He knows I cannot tell him. . . ." [19]

[17] "A Sermon on Commemoration of the Lady Danvers, Late Wife of Sir John Danvers" (1627).

[18] Blake Smith.

[19] Donne, "St. Paul's. Easter Day. April 13th, 1628." *LXXX Sermons* (23), 1640.

At the point of beginning, faith has no choice but to be "bluntly biological" about death. There are concessions to be made, or else there are evasions to be explained.

Death is not sleep; it is more, and deeper, and darker.

If death be but a sleepe, yet it is a sleepe that an earth-quake cannot wake. . . .[20] And what is so intricate, so intangling as death? Who ever got out of a winding sheet? And what is so heavy as death? Who ever threw off his grave stone? [21]

Death is not sleep; it is heavier, and darker, and deeper.

Death sweeps clean as it goes. It leaves nothing behind it to speak a word of meaning or of hope.

The ashes of an Oak in the Chimney, are no Epitaph of that Oak, to tell me how high or how large that was; it tels me not what flocks it sheltered while it stood, nor what men it hurt when it fell. The dust of great persons graves is speechlesse too, it sayes nothing, it distinguishes nothing.[22]

Death is without mercy; nothing that lives can evade it for long, and the more complex the living thing is, the higher its form of life, the more vulnerable is it to death. That is to say, death is the "most terrible and the only evil." [23] Even the notion that death can be conquered through birth is an illusion, for this has nothing to do with personality; birth is

[20] Donne, "The fourth of my Prebend Sermons upon my five Psalms: Preached at S. Pauls, 28. Ianuary, 1626 [1626/7]."

[21] Donne, "Preached to the King at White-hall, upon the occasion of the Fast, April 5, 1628."

[22] Donne, "At Whitehall, 1st Friday in Lent, March 8, 1621/2," *LXXX Sermons* (15), 1640.

[23] Berdyaev, *The Destiny of Man*, p. 320.

concerned only with the continuation of species, not individuals. So death is the final, ultimate evil. He poses the constant threat of meaninglessness over the highest hopes and most enduring enterprises. He denies any and all fellowship, communion, unity, and togetherness. He makes all tenure temporary, all victory empty, all wholeness partial, and all endeavor pointless. Death wins everything! This faith concedes, and this is why faith makes death its central problem; this is why faith's ultimate claim must deal with death. This is also the key to the qualitative distinction between Christian ethics and any other level of ethics. To faith there is no valid ethic that does not face, admit, defeat, and pass by death.

Therefore, faith is an advance over all other ethical systems. The ancient Hebrews knew nothing of *personal* immortality, for they knew too little of personal self-consciousness. This is why the concept of individual redemption is still so foreign to Israel. Only in Job does a note of personal destiny and its tragic nature come to stature. Is this why the ethic of Judaism never claimed the higher levels beyond legalism to grace and creativeness? [24] Both the Stoic and the Buddhist are impotent in the face of death. They issue death no challenge and can offer no level of ethic beyond the level of conformity. Yet this is beyond the reach of that naturalism which acts as if there were no death. Such an attitude lifts nothing and no one. In other thought schools death is allowed for; the materialists, the so-called positivists, and others even discuss death, then try to put it "out of sight, out of mind." They have no "memory of death" and therefore build with gravestones, unfeelingly, unknowingly, insensate, and shallow.

[24] See the levels of ethics in *ibid*.

Everyone else counsels resignation, submission to fate. The Christian faith alone has an adequate grasp of sin and evil, but this arises as a by-product of its confrontation of death. In this framework sin is an explanation of death, and the concept of sin arose in this manner and will die only when that which it arose to confront dies. In brief, sin is the Christian means of explaining death. In no other religion does sin take on the proportions it assumes in the Christian faith, and in no other ethic is the problem of death central. This is why the Christian incarnation is unique.

The Christian faith alone faces death, bluntly and biologically. It explains death with sin and overcomes it with incarnation, but this does not explain the death of the nonmoral. Hence, the Christian doctrine of the incompleteness of creation comes to bear tremendous weight. Here at the concept of death is the center. Around this hub revolves all the meaning of faith. This is the central problem; this is where the seams come together to make the fabric a whole. The concepts of salvation-sin, redemption-evil, are by-stations on the way to an explanation of death. Death is encountered, won, broken by incarnation, but the whole redemptive enterprise hinges on the sovereignty of that God whose creative work remains unfinished (process), whose redemptive work is an incident on the road to complete creation (person), whose highest sovereignty is to be achieved in the completion of all he has begun and is doing (purpose).

Process

Whenever a man of faith begins so confidently, announces so boldly, what he hopes to do, there surges up in seeking

135

hearts the expectancy that perhaps this man can do it, can tell you about it. In this confident beginning you are thrilled with the thought of some impossible good fortune. And you think he is going to tell you the magic meaning, but most times he tells you nothing. This is because faith can promise you nothing but faith, and what faith learns as she goes. Only one of our number has been "there" and returned, but we know him only by faith, too. What has faith learned from him and from the journey?

Plotinus spoke of a "sense of the yonder" and said it is native to us, a part of our nature. We know it as an innate urge to completeness, a sense of something still to come, a "sense of the yonder." Under its influence we seldom will admit that life is full; there is always "more." This magic feel for the future makes a man at eighty-five wonder what wonders are yonder that he has not reached. So, Sophocles at ninety writes *Oedipus;* Leo XIII achieves his highest good after seventy; Titian[25] is eighty-five when he closes his brass doors on the sacristy at St. Mark's. This urge to completeness made Benjamin Franklin plenipotentiary to the court of France at seventy-two, a member of the peace commission to Britain at seventy-five, and president of the executive council of Pennsylvania from seventy-nine to eighty-one years of age. The urge to completeness, the awareness of process, keeps a man from feeling that life is finished. At ninety years Elihu Root took the lead in some top-flight statesmanship, and Oliver Wendell Holmes, George Albert Coe, Barney Baruch,

[25] Tiziano Vecelli, d. 1576.

Henry Ford, Toscanini, and Herbert Hoover, to name a few, came to new and great heights after the eightieth birthday.

The urge to completeness is, perhaps, more accurately described as a sense of incompleteness. The sense of process, event still to happen, leads to the conclusion that the incompleteness is general. Nothing is completed. Creation, unfinished, continues! Not even God has completed his initial creative urge. God's creation is yet an incomplete creation *at which he still is working.* When God processed man in the midst of circumstances that involved man's choice, God had not finished creating. Nor did he become a mere curious spectator to the forces and demons man has built by his choices. Instead, he has continued as a creative personality within the frame of human history. Nor is his creative work exhausting.

Our God is not out of breath, because he hath blown one tempest, and swallowed a Navy: Our God hath not burnt out his eyes, because he hath looked upon a Train of Powder.[26]

He, God, remains in positive, active, creative relation with his creatures; his creative activity never ceases. The Sabbath of the Creator is an activity continuing with and in his children for whom the great word remains "potential," the sense of becoming.

Now faith says that man bears the mark of the eternal, the *imago dei,* the divine image. This is to say right off that man is two. He is of dual nature and hence of dual capacities. Made in the image of God means "made with an infinite potential." Man, crown of creation, is Somebody.

---

[26] Donne, Sermon XXV in *Passages from Twenty-six Sermons.*

It is too little to call *Man a little world; Except God, Man* is a *diminutive* to nothing. Man consistes of more pieces, more parts, than the world. . . . And if those pieces were extended. . . , Man would bee the *Gyant,* and the Worlde the *Dwarfe.* . . . the *Aire* would be too litle for this *Orbe* of Man to move in, the firmament would bee but enough for this Starre.[27]

But this somebody-man is somebody more on the basis of his capacity for "becoming" than on the biological level already accomplished. Man is never wholly generated biologically; he is more. There must be a second womb or you are a half-born man.

The faith says man is incomplete, God is still creating, and that God has a realized idea of what man is like when he is complete. The faith says God cuts through the strands of human history in an incarnation, an enfleshing, to make a demonstration of what man is like when he is completed. God's idea, his realized demonstration, is Jesus Christ, Redeemer, Son of God, *monogenes* (only one of his kind), who invades history as its Master and finished product not only to demonstrate but to make completion possible. More bluntly put, he makes creation and our suffering make sense by giving it a goal, *raison d'être*. But what is more, he comes into history to bring to half-born men the *power for becoming.*

This "power for becoming" captured the writer of John's Gospel as no other. Of all the sacred writings John and Ephesians hold the most for us, of this *process* in which we are involved. In some sense the highest peak of spiritual insight the race has known was reached in the climax of John's prologue (1:1-14). He begins with the tremendous dualism

[27] Donne, *Devotions,* IV.

innate in history: light and dark; life and death; then says there is a Word over it all who is there wherever you choose to begin: but the Word came into history, *was fleshed,* and we saw him, and everytime we passed him, something of his grace spilled over on us (grace upon grace). Then comes the insight of process and becoming:

"As many as received him, to them gave he power
    to become the sons of God"

—but there is a better translation. When one preserves in English the Greek verb action and time, it reads:

To everyone who took him in (once for all as if to keep forever) *in them did he release* (once for all) *the power to go on becoming Godlike.*

Power to become, and it comes to faith from the Christ. This is the urge to completeness as the gospel knows it. And this is that urge which all human life shares and for which all nonmoral life exists. To this must be related all endeavor and search, all inquiry and advancement, in all the areas of creation. It is to this urge and its potential that death and its frustrations, life and its limitations, which are little deaths, stand opposed. Only the urge to become, out of the sense of process and potential, stands opposed to death. If there are no process and no potential, death is already victor. But the urge, and the process, and the potential are there. Sometimes they express themselves in words like these, written late at night in a blister on the side of the atomic pile at Oak Ridge; for even a physicist knows the "urge to become."

Men of old—before my time and age—
Heard their God speak
from a burning bush;
Or heard His mighty summons
roll down to Earth on the shoulders
of the storm.
With power He spoke—they moved
To bend their minds, their lives
to that Cause for which they
had, unknowing, come.

But in my day—a less heroic age—
No blinding flash of sun heralds
the man turned to His path;
No tongue of flame licks out to
sear its message on my brain—
Out of deathly quiet, out of a soundless
universe, a word is formed for me.
Yet, whether with dissonant fury or
with soft, harmonic notes the call
shall sound,
It still requires as answer the passion
of a man,
And I must set myself to serve the
God whose moving finger traces on my heart
the word, "Become!" [28]

This is the urge and the power that overcomes death. Faith simply says *death is part of the process of becoming,* no more. To this process life belongs, but death belongs too; it is a part of the process. It is not final; it does not have the last

[28] By Milton Marney. Used by permission.

word. While it is a manifestation against life, the fact of its presence alone gives depth to the meaning of life. The meaning is tied to the boundary. Man's last hope is uttered with respect to death, and this means that evil has the last word in life. Its greatness and terror spill over into all our living rooms, and it keeps us from this world's expectations.

Death carries over into living and is a normal part of life. Every day we die a little. All normal children, however hard we work to keep them little, look forward to growing up. And death is a part of the growth. My little girls weep every May because they cannot have this year's teachers next year. They look forward to growing up, and yet they die a little bit in each journey. For that is the meaning of death—separation a bit at a time, a moment and a place. It appears again when we have spent some days in some beautiful mountain refuge. I have heard them, leaning out the car windows to cry, "Good-by, little house!" "Good-by, pretty trees!" They mean that they are experiencing death—the reluctant separation from part of yourself, the sloughing off of things you would keep if you could. But it is a part of growing up, too. Death is part; it is written into life.

This explains the strange double view of death the faith supports. Since death is part of the process, growth comes only with death. The urge to completeness calls for growth which comes only at the cost of death. Hence death is both feared and loved, both hated and desired. "Welcome, Sister Death," cried the Saint of Assisi, but it was to him an entry into a larger room.

Death is in birth and life, but the childlike desire to grow up makes death endurable. " 'Except ye become as little chil-

141

dren,' except you can wake on your fiftieth birthday with the same forward-looking excitement and interest in life that you enjoyed when you were five, 'you cannot see the Kingdom of God.' " [29] That is, death is a part of the process if life is good, but if you have organized life around your own petty little hates, discords, and prejudices, life is full of death, a hell on wheels, and no faith in any process can reach you. In faith that sees death as part of a process a man comes to the very end of his life still carrying on the adventure. Lynn Harold Hough reminds us that Anselm was quite eager to get over into the other world since he could settle some matters better there than in this world.

Person

Before the turn of the century one wild morning's work by Vigilantes filled a corner of Boothill with new graves in a little gold-rush town high in a Montana valley. Now the traveler can still read names, a date, and the legend "hanged"; and that is all; except for one stone. It adds a word:

Peccavi

I have sinned! Strange-sounding Latin word for those rude days in those raw hills—who knew it? Why is it on only one grave? Who is this Haze Lyons, Hanged, in September, who says "Peccavi"? I have sinned! Who is this fellow who lies there confessing his sins to the world? How is it that he must confess his sins so long, and is "Peccavi" his last word? And did he know what it meant to say "Peccavi"?

[29] Dorothy Sayers, *Creed or Chaos?* (London: Methuen & Co., Ltd., 1947), p. 15.

He is not just a sinful being expiating his sin. He is not merely one social animal cut off by a rope and some stones from his fellows. He is not just a once animate thing caught between his conscious and his unconscious striving for an unworthy goal. He is a creative being—cut off.

Nor is he just a man. He is *everybody*. He is not a fragment, a section, a pea in a pod. He is all, he is each, he is every. He is a riddle and contains in him the meaning of the universe. He is a microcosm, a whole world-full of meaning. He is a "diminutive to nothing, except God."

The Koreans bury their dead in a sitting position, arms clasped around knees; they pile up cairns of rock and earth like huge blisters in the sides of rough hills. We stretch our dead out flat in rows or put their ashes in orderly little caches in devised caves. Certain Indian tribes tied their dead to swaying platforms high in the branches of trees. Not long since, missionaries found some of their African converts had broken open the new coffin before the ceremonies of interment and had partially eaten the person of their dead fellow to keep his strength alive in the tribe. Why are we *all* so careful about the disposition of our dead? Why do we not dispose of the inevitable without muss or fuss or sentiment? And why do we call it "civilized" to preserve so carefully that that has already gone from us?

Every person is a unique and unrepeatable event. He happened once, and there is no way completely to obliterate his memory from the mass mind. The race remembers. He is indestructible because he is an event. He happened once.

In this sense every person is an *Incarnation*. He is an enfleshing of spiritual values, unique, eternal, unrepetitive. He

143

really does not happen again, though he may share trends and characteristics enough for us to categorize him as "good," "bad," or "indifferent." In each there resides an unbelievable potential, never fully achieved, never completely denied. This potential is the creation of God; it is not generated by the biological process. Rather, it is God's "idea," to be realized in time. That is to say, *faith must make a distinction between individuality and personality.*

The distinction that must be made between individuality and personality, though vastly involved, can be clearly delineated. All individualism arises out of an improper view of the self; all personality is contained in the capacity for community which individualism per se can never know. And most significantly, the power of personality against death rises precisely out of this capacity for communion that mere individualism can never know.

Somewhere Thomas Carlyle described the awe-filled nights when seventy-two Chateaus "flamed aloft in the Maconnais and Beaujolais alone," [30] and prefaced the uproar with, "Did ye mark among your Rights of Man, that man was not to die of starvation, while there was bread reaped by him? It is among the Mights of Man." [31] And there is a might of personality, too. Even though death stands athwart our way, it is a might of personality to *take* the bread of eternal life He has reaped. There is a might within personality that refuses death; it treats death as the unendurable. The watchword is, "I will not submit!" This might is the source of the rejection of death. Death is a tragic enemy only where per-

[30] *Op. cit.,* p. 179.
[31] *Ibid.*

sonality knows itself to be personality; but wherever personality is personality, it knows of eternity and immortality and will not give in to less. There is no tragedy in the temporal or transitory; tragedy arises out of the threat to the eternally valuable. It is only when the assertion of individuality is transposed by Love into the realization of personality that both the threat of death and the possibility of overcoming death can be seen together. In view of the threat and the possibility, personality examines its "might" and originates its struggle. For struggle is involved. Personality itself arises out of the conflict between death and my potential.

Personality is, then, a task to be achieved. The means of achieving the task is wrapped up in a *creative* ethic through which we are called not to the procreation of invalid temporal and earthy concerns, but to the *creation* of enduring, immortal values that are fit for the kingdom of God. The source of our personality is the kingdom of God from whence come the moral dignity and freedom which are our might in the task achieved *by means of Christian ethics:* the involvement in struggle of a being capable of eternal choices who achieves his eternity in his victories over the temporal. The goal of Christian ethics is not the kingdom of God; it is Christian personality, a task to be achieved. The kingdom is both source and habitat of Christian personality; but God makes the kingdom, not the totaled efforts of men on the road to becoming personality. Personality, then, is the maturing of a process which includes and passes death. Its converse, its alternate, is *waste,* waste of the most precious thing God created, his *idea,* his possibility of communion with realized human potential.

Personality is, further, a communion to be established—in

itself a denial of death. Its converse is individuality, which is, when projected, a solipsism, an utter loneliness, which is hell. Only personality can know communion. Individuality cannot know community; it reaches its ceiling this side of any social good. But man, made for community, able to commune, cannot resist the calls to community, and this is the hallmark of personality, the task to be achieved. That is to say, the kingdom of God is the community of achieved personality, and this is the denial of death which cannot exist with communion.

Personality is more. It is a calling to be consummated. This involves God and destroys death, for the two are incompatible. Its alternate is purposelessness, which devalues life and leaves it in the grave. The tragedy of perverted vocation is the tragedy of our lost human potential. This *is* the grave. "The majority of men do never really manage in their whole life to be more than they were in childhood and youth." This Christian calling to be consummated in Christian personality is nothing more than the realization of the God image in man's potential. Once more the means is Christian ethics, and in this context of calling the content of the ethic is Christian love. That is to say, our calling is to be a *giver of life*. Within this calling Christian personality is to

act so as to conquer death and affirm everywhere . . . eternal and immortal life. It is base to forget the death of a single living being and to be reconciled to it. The death of the least and most miserable creature is unendurable. . . . All and everything must be raised to eternal life. . . . Man must always and in everything be a giver of life. . . . Love for all that lives, for every creature, rising

146

above the love for abstract ideas, means struggle against death in the name of eternal life.[32]

Personality is invulnerable. "Man is not meant, forsooth, to grow from the ground like a mushroom, quickly to perish away on the spot of ground that begot him, leaving no trace behind of himself and his animate actions." [33] From the beginning the faith has been one with the hope. The seventy years have always been a prelude to something immeasurably larger and grander. To Christian ears the funeral finale is an opening overture. But, to us, this is true only and because of

"Jesus Christ, the faithful witness, the first-born
of the dead, and the ruler of kings on earth"
(Rev. 1:5a R.S.V.).

He it is whom we have believed to be able to make all things new. The "faithful witness" is truth; the "first-born of the dead" is destiny. The "ruler of kings on earth" is the principle of order in history. But this brings up the discussion of that purpose with which the answer of faith must be content for a time. Meantime,

He comes to us as One unknown, without a name, as of old, by the lake-side, He came to those men who knew Him not. He speaks to us the same word: "Follow thou Me!" and sets us to the tasks which He has to fulfil for our time. He commands. And to those who obey Him, whether they be wise or simple, He

[32] Berdyaev, *The Destiny of Man*, p. 322. Used by permission of Geoffrey Bles Ltd. See also Albert Schweitzer, *Out of My Life and Thought* (New York: Henry Holt & Co., 1949), pp. 269 ff.

[33] Goethe, *Hermann and Dorothea*, p. 75.

will reveal Himself in the toils, the conflicts, the sufferings which they shall pass through in His fellowship, and, as an ineffable mystery, *they shall learn in their own experience Who He is.*[34]

Purpose

Whatever the purpose may be, it must include the whole of the universe. To what purpose are those 5,000,000,000 years sent? What is God making? To what purpose were these creatures, these wild experiments of nature with forty-foot necks? And what continuation of that purpose turned them into lizards to scurry away from my boot on the canyon floor? What is that Virgo I am told is 22,000,000 light-years away, and what does it mean to say it is 1,000,000,000 light-years from a point there to a point there? If this macrocosm is so vast, what of the still unexplored vastness of the microcosms where there may be as much space between matter as in the whole stellar system itself on a comparable basis? To what intent is all this stuff, this energy, this space, and vast, dark, secret time, and what is light?

Is it waste? Is it purposeless void proceeding to purposeless void? Is it a grave with both ends knocked out? Then what is this sense of order and cosmos? What is the meaning of process? And what is communication, and value, and beauty, and consciousnesss, and knowledge, and memory?

Here obtrudes the unquenchable human-Christian egoism about man. We will not believe God intends to waste it all—not even the suffering our ego has brought us. We believe he has done it again with respect to man in that he has wrapped

---

[34] Schweitzer, *The Quest of the Historical Jesus* (London: A. & C. Black Ltd., 1922), p. 401. (Italics mine.)

up his purpose in very small packages of life which he has hidden on an inconsequential speck in the periphery of the suns. We say that he has said to a finite, diseased, and dying two-legged biped, "You have an illimitable potential; multiply and get dominion over it all!" We do not know what others may be like us or our earth. We say there may well be 100,000,000 inhabited blobs like ours. We do not know, but we believe of ourselves that we can know and that we will know. So we speak of plastic balloons two hundred miles up in the summer sky, we "photograph" space vehicles from other stars, we talk of way stations on the way to Mars, and we can say what stuff comprises the dead corpses of those worlds that float around us. We look through glass to the worlds of space above us and the worlds of bacilli beneath us, and we know we are *middlemen, bourgeois,* on our way up, bound to have dominion. And we believe that all knowledge, all inquiry and search, physico-biochemical search, metaphysico-psychological search, historico-sociological search, have a spiritual end and a religious meaning far beyond our powers of dreaming or imagination.

We believe that history itself is creative, that it makes things that did not exist before. We see history as *actual* and will not be diverted from our sense of reality here. We say history has value; it is not a pointless, whirling concatenation of atoms which blindly run. We believe that the *subjective factor of history* (God) and the transformation of meaning that is his process at work includes temporal events like ourselves in an eternal *order*.[35] This is why we can believe in

---

[35] See Robinson's five characteristics of history in *op. cit.,* p. xxvi.

the God who is in history, and in this faith, upon which we bet our lives, we, here and there, get such a glimpse beyond that our hearts exult.

> Now is the winter of our discontent
> Made glorious summer. . . .[36]

for a while, at least.

In the light of the process in which we are involved, the persons we are, and the purpose God follows, we will not accept that death.

> Oh dreadful thought, if all our sires and we,
> Are but foundations of a race to be.[37]

No, we cannot accept it, that the "stars do blindly run." We see purpose in our defeats and our deaths, and by our strange brand of faith's logic cry that the blindness and the fault are ours.

> The angels keep their ancient places;—
> Turn but a stone and start a wing!
> 'Tis ye, 'tis your estrangèd faces,
> That miss the many-splendoured thing.[38]

We believe that earth's concerns have consequence beyond us, and the converse, that that high purpose for this whole cosmos must ultimately be worked out in us and on earth, and elsewhere.

Christianity has taught us, says Kierkegaard, "to think

---

[36] Shakespeare, *King Richard III*, Act I, scene 1.

[37] Dixon, *op. cit.*, p. 189. Used by permission of Edward Arnold & Co. and St. Martin's Press.

[38] Francis Thompson.

dauntlessly of everything earthly and worldly including death.[39] In this faith that process proceeds, personality is paramount, and God is purposive and powerful, we cry:

> "Laugh with me at this Babylon
> that laughs at us."

We believe God made nothing that he means to let go forever, although faith keeps warning us how difficult it is to let the self go. For when faith says it "knows," it does not know what it is talking about. Even the Christ had to faith his way through death. Who would refuse to die for the sins of the world for three days if he knew he would rise? He faithed his way; he pulled no rank on us! The heresy of our time is not that we preach Christ as if he were not God; it is, rather, that we preach Jesus as if he were not man. He faithed that the purpose of God would bring him through, and the Christian faith hangs on what the Father did!

We have to faith it, too. This means we hang our destiny on what we cannot know. We bet our lives that God has an eternal purpose which involves Christ and us. In that faith

> "Something above the wreck is steady still." [40]

And therefore, we act as if we hear the divine call to become participators in the drama of becoming; we seek to live redemptively and creatively, with our eyes on his high purpose as we understand it. As we go, we know we already share a kingdom of God within which we are constantly seeing death happen and just as constantly refusing its hold on any-

[39] *The Sickness unto Death* (Princeton, N. J.: Princeton University Press, 1941), pp. 12, 13.
[40] John Masefield.

thing that lived or lives. And even when we are eighty-seven and already aware that the final physical despair is upon us, we are also aware of the reams of work we have yet to do; we are still wondering what, in God's name, we and our fellows can become. And one day we lead our last prayer in chapel, and it goes: "O God, let these young men know what thou art doing, in order that they may be doing the same thing." [41] And our faith is secure enough "that neither death, whensoever it shall come, may seeme terrible; nor life tedious, how long soever it shall last." [42]

Sometimes, once in a great while, we have a premonition of the voyage and take a temporary farewell of those we love. Whoever did it better than John Donne in the last paragraph of the last sermon he preached?

There wee leave you in that blessed *dependancy to hang* upon *him* that *hangs* upon the *Crosse*, there *bath* in his *teares*, there *suck* at his *woundes*, and *lie downe in peace* in his *grave*, till hee *vouchsafe* you a *resurrection*, and an *ascension* into that *King-dome*, which hee hath *purchas'd for you*, with the *inestimable price* of his *incorruptible blood*. Amen.

[41] W. O. Carver.
[42] Richard Redmer in the publisher's preface to the first edition (1632) of *Death's Duell*, Donne's last sermon.

152

DEBIT

If you have met Doubt, that half magician who cannot quiet the ghosts he raises, if you are a question asker (how inane to deal with questions no one asks) this *Faith in Conflict* could have become a caravan for you, for it has dealt with doubt and conflict and questions. But if you do not sleep with doubt and if you have no questions, it could never be more than carrousel, a caravan with music that goes no place.

I hope, too, that you are a reader. If so, while reading my score you have heard over your shoulder, from nearby and in the distance, the voices of singers who have sung it well indeed. Where I have known whose music I sing, I have said so, in the hope it would send you to a clear singer. But there are some whose music I have used as if it were my own, as indeed it is. I took it from them at the price of a diligent ear:

Wolfgang Goethe and
Friedrich Nietzsche
Nikolai Berdyaev and
Søren Kierkegaard
W. Macneile Dixon and
John Donne
Fyodor Dostoevsky and
Paul Tillich
William Temple and
G. B. Shaw
Radoslav Tsanoff and
Reinhold Niebuhr
Emil Brunner, Martin Luther,
and Alfred North Whitehead

And there are other kinds of music: the *allegro maestoso* of debate with W. J. Kilgore, F. N. Ginascol, Blake Smith, and my brother, Milton, whose poem I have used on page 140; and the *andante sostenuto* of devoted efficiency sung by Irma Ferguson, who now knows the entire score by heart. If you should find somewhere a passage that has any depth or color, it likely has been lifted from that rich and even syncopated *larghetto grandioso* of the life I live with a woman of incalculable faith and our daughters.

INDEX OF NAMES

Copernicus, 91
Corvo, Frederick baron, 21
Cosette in *Les Miserables,* 41
Coulton, G. G., 16
Crito, 91
Crowfoot, 129
Cyprian, 81

Darrow, Clarence, 13-14
Darwin, Charles, 13, 22, 92-93
Darwin, Erasmus, 93
Descartes, 91-92
Dewey, John, 22, 95
Dickie, E. P., 18, 21, 26 n., 31, 48
Divine, Father, 63
Dixon, 97 n., 98, 101, 150
Donne, John, 131, 132, 133, 137, 138, 152-53
Dostoevsky, Fyodor, 16, 17, 18, 23, 47-48, 51, 60-61, 69
Durant, Will, 17, 126

Einstein, 15, 22
Eisenhower, 117
Eliot, T. S., 58

Fairbairn, Andrew M., 31, 73
Falstaff in *Henry IV,* 55
Faust, 14, 21, 123
Feuerbach, 72
Ford, Henry, 137
Francis of Assisi, 129, 141
Franklin, Benjamin, 136
Fredegonda, 125
Frederick, Barbarossa, 16
Frederick II, Emperor, 16
Freud, Sigmund, 22, 72, 93

Galilei, Galileo, 17, 91
Gifford Lectures, 98
Goethe, 21, 48, 51, 54, 78, 123, 147
Gogol, 67
Gwynn, Nell, 129

156

Hal, Prince, in *Henry IV,* 54
Hannibal, 117
Harnack, 72
Harry in *Family Reunion,* 58
Harry in *Henry IV,* 126
Hauge, Bud, 46
Hawkins, Sir John, 47
Hegel, 92, 94
Heine, Heinrich, 52, 61
Henry IV in *Henry IV,* 55, 126
Herodotus, 50
Hitler, 32, 88, 117
Holmes, Oliver Wendell, 126
Homer, 95
Hoover, Herbert, 137
Horton, Walter Marshall, 18
Hotspur in *Henry IV,* 126
Hough, Lynn Harold, 142
Hugo, Victor, 42
Hutchins, Merrill, 105
Hutton, Sir John, 48
Huxley, T. H., 21 n., 93

Isaiah, 114

Job, 134
John, the evangelist, 129
Johnson, Euclid, 46
Josephus, 50

Kant, 26, 52
Kepler, 91
Khan, Genghis, 117
Kierkegaard, 57, 80, 116, 150-51
Kingsley, Charles, 21

Labadie, Jean de, 63
Laplace, Pierre Simon de, 92
Le Comte, Edward S., 129
Leibniz, 21, 92
Lenin, 52
Leo I, 89
Leo XIII, 136